Wild Weekend Diet

THE DIET WORKSHOP
Wild Weekend Diet

LOIS LINDAUER

*THE DIET WORKSHOP is a registered trademark of
The Diet Workshop, Inc., Brookline, Massachusetts.*

DELACORTE PRESS/NEW YORK

Published by
Delacorte Press
1 Dag Hammarskjold Plaza
New York, N.Y. 10017

Manufactured in the United States of America

First printing—March 1985

Library of Congress Cataloging in Publication Data

Lindauer, Lois Lyons.
     The Diet Workshop® wild weekend diet.

     1. Reducing diets—Recipes.   2. Low-calorie diet—
Recipes.   I. The Diet Workshop, Inc.   II. Title.
RM222.2.L479   1985   613.2'5
ISBN 0-385-29383-6
Library of Congress Catalog Card Number: 84–19933

Contents

Acknowledgments

To Kathy Ettinger, who researched painstakingly, to Donna Roazen, who commented and suggested carefully, and to Laura Warren, who picked up the pieces, I am grateful.

Wild Weekend Diet

Introduction

This book is dedicated to the understanding that for most people, the most consistent turn-on in their lives is food. Think about it . . . how many people, activities, or possessions do you find more exciting than food?

Food is a reliable comfort. Food is easy to find and eating is easy to do. The process is almost automatic; it's the button we push for solace, for relief of boredom, for joy, for sociability, and—oh, yes—for hunger.

Given a choice of being fat or thin, you'd probably opt for thin. It's when you're given a choice between thin and a chocolate sundae that the choosing gets hard! To reconcile the excitement of eating to the visual image you'd like for yourself is not simple. Or easy. It's the ever-present battle between long-term goals versus short-term gratification.

It's easy to fail on a diet. Everybody does at some time or other. Food pushers everywhere love a diet failure. They stand ready and willing to remind others that it's "only normal," to forget one's resolves. Watching you fall off the diet wagon relieves their guilt about their own failures.

Sophie Tucker said, "I've been rich and I've been poor, and believe me, rich is better." You've probably experienced fat and thin in your life and know that thin is better.

Thin is better than beer at a football game.
Thin is better than franks at home plate.

Thin is better than popcorn at the movies.

Thin is better than apple pie a la mode or Reese's Peanut Butter Cups.

Thin is better than Sara Lee Cheesecake.

Thin is better than McDonald's french fries.

Thin is best!

And you can be thin!

If any of the above activities and/or foods especially speak to you, be of good cheer: you need not banish them from your life forever. What you must do is incorporate the reality that you can't have everything all the time. You've got to make choices. Every day. Every meal. And you can elect to enjoy your special foods. But not all the time.

And that's what this book is about.

Lois Lindauer

CHAPTER 1

TGIF

In the best of all possible diet worlds there would be no weekends. Without the temptation of Saturdays and Sundays most of us would stay with a diet for seven days a week, lose our weight, and get thin.

Well, that's how it works in the best of all possible diet worlds. Now let's talk about life as it really is.

Most people find it hard to diet on the weekends; maybe the following problems are familiar to you. If you eat at a friend's or at a relative's house, you may have no choices. If you eat in a restaurant, you probably have too many choices. If you stay at home, you may feel lonely or bored, and, possibly, sorry for yourself, feelings that rank high among diet killers.

Whatever the reason, whatever the season, there is no doubt that Saturday night is the hungriest night of the week. The iron resolve you made on Monday crumbles to rusty sawdust on Saturday when the siren sings ever so sweetly of lasagna, piña coladas, Chateaubriand, or———. Fill in your own food Frankenstein.

At last here is a diet that meets the Saturday night challenge head-on. It is called the Wild Weekend Diet, and with it you will scale weekend hurdles, steer effortlessly through the weekend obstacle course, and come to a triumphant rest at your weight goal.

What makes a weekend wild?

Well, dieter, if you can eat pizza or beef bourguignon or blueberry cheesecake and still lose weight, that, to us, is wild.

On the Wild Weekend Diet your need to be sociable and to enjoy your food on Saturday night is recognized and taken care of. Or, if you elect to stay home and eat fun foods, that's okay, too. Whatever the circumstance, you'll be eating food you love, food that satisfies heart and soul, as well as the stomach. Foods like shrimp scampi or a foot-long hot dog. Drinks like sombreros or frozen daiquiris. Whatever you want, it's yours.

On the Wild Weekend Diet you can have your cake, eat it, and still lose weight!

How Was the Wild Weekend Diet Created?

Since 1965 The Diet Workshop has learned from hundreds of thousands of dieters that people will succeed on a diet and reach goal weight only if they feel satisfied. It is our experience that the dieter who feels deprived is the dieter who falls off the wagon. After that, Humpty Dumpty takes over, and the diet never gets back together again. We also found that the people who enjoy what they're eating can stay on a diet indefinitely and that they do get thin!

How Did We Discover This Phenomenon?

At first we experimented with a small and very skeptical group of dieters. We encouraged them to "take the weekend off." And when they did so, we found that they stuck longer to their diets *and* reached their goals to a greater degree than those of the control group who were *not* treated to a weekend off.

One of our dieters, Marie L., was terrified at first at the thought of "going off" on the weekend. She thought she would just "blow her diet" as she had many times in the past. But then she decided to trust the experience of The Diet Workshop and go along with the experiment.

"On my weekend off," says Marie, "I made plans to go to my favorite French restaurant. It's the kind that makes its own bread. In the past, when I visited this restaurant while I was dieting, this visit did the diet in. I would start out resolved not to eat any bread, and then I'd sit there and watch others eat and feel so deprived that I finally decided to forget my diet 'just for the evening,' and eat the bread, and then I'd get so depressed at giving in, that was the end of my diet.

"On the Wild Weekend Diet," Marie continues, "I selected my favorite appetizer, entrée, and dessert, and had *four* pieces of bread. Because these foods were built into my eating plan, I knew I was 'diet-safe,' and I finished my week of dieting with a whopping four-pound loss."

Susan B. is an executive whose pressure-filled job calls for a lot of weekend traveling. "I find," says Susan, "that the best way for me to unwind after a day on the road is to eat a substantial dinner and have a few drinks. As a matter of fact, I blame my expense account for the ten pounds I gained in the first ten months of my job, as well as the twenty I put on in the next two years."

Susan credits the Wild Weekend Diet for giving her the knowledge and incentive to take off those unwanted pounds and for keeping her thin for the last twelve months. "I eat prime rib every Saturday night along with a baked potato and sour cream and two martinis. Looking forward to my Saturday night dinner keeps me on balance and keeps me thin, too. My appearance is very important to me and to my position. Looking good has helped my sales, and best of all, I find that the pressure of my job is much easier to handle when I don't have to also worry about the pressures of dieting and being overweight."

Satisfied that we had a formula that everyone could follow with successful results, we are now ready to share this new and revolutionary way to lose weight with you.

How Does It Work?

As you probably know, most recommended diets provide about 1,200 calories a day for women and 1,500 for men. These calories are portioned out over three meals and snacks, each meal containing protein, such as fish, chicken, meat, cheese, or eggs; and a carbohydrate, such as bread, potato, rice, and starchy vegetables. Fruits and milk each day are also part of these eating plans.

The arithmetic is simple: 1,200 calories per day for women, 1,500 calories per day for men, when multiplied by the seven days of the week, gives us a total of 8,400 calories per week for women, 10,500 calories for men.

Instead of portioning the calories out evenly during the week—1,200 daily for women, 1,500 for men—the Wild Weekend Diet allows approximately half of the week's calories from Monday through Friday and the remaining calories on the two weekend days.

The Wild Weekend Diet is a balanced diet, and you will still control your *weekly* amount of food, but you eat sparingly during the week, so that you can eat your food favorites on the weekend.

And Here's Some More Information

Monday through Friday, the diet you follow is structured and simple. Because of this simplicity you will not have to count calories; that has been done for you. Each day that you follow this weekday plan, you save hundreds of calories, which you then spend as you choose on the weekend. From apple pie to zabaglione, all foods are available for your choosing. And, most important, at the end of each and every week you lose weight.

A Calorie Is a Calorie Is a Calorie

This is true.

The calories in lettuce count in the exact same way as the calories in lasagna. It will not, however, astonish you to hear that there are many more calories in lasagna.

The point of this information is to let you know that your body can burn up only a limited number of calories each day. If you exceed your body's ability to burn up calories in the food you eat, these calories accumulate in your body as fat. If you eat less than your calorie burn-up rate, you will burn up your body fat and lose weight.

The Wild Weekend Diet is planned so that over the seven days of the week, your total calorie intake is below your body's calorie maintenance level. Therefore, you create a calorie deficit and lose weight.

There is one principle that holds true for every diet you have ever been on or ever read about. If you eat fewer calories than you burn up, you will lose weight. On the Wild Weekend Diet you eat less per week than your body requires, with the result that you get thinner each week.

As on other balanced eating plans, weight loss results for the first week of dieting is about 3 to 5 pounds for women, 4 to 7 pounds for men. On each succeeding week weight loss averages out to about half the amount lost in week one. So, if you have 25 pounds to lose and you're a woman, it will take you about three months of healthy Wild Weekend dieting for you to reach your goal.

There may come a time, of course, when you are faced by that old diet bugaboo, plateaus. When you do, remember our promise to you: If you keep on dieting you'll keep on losing. The weight loss may not show up on the scale exactly at the moment you want and/or expect it to, but you will get the result you're looking for if you are confident about what you're doing and you *stay with it.*

We deal with that special plateau, the one that occurs when you're about 10 pounds from your goal and most anxious to lose weight, in Chapter 11, "The Last Ten Pounds Plus Best Diet Tips." The suggestions there will work well any time you're going through a plateau during your weight-loss process and want quick results.

The Wild Weekend Checking Account

The Wild Weekend Diet works just like your checking account. Consider your calorie allotment as your "salary." If you are a woman, your salary is 8,400 calories weekly; if you're a man, your stipend is 10,500 calories. Each of these calorie allotments provides for a calorie *deficit* at the end of the week, which means that you burn up your fat and get thinner.

From a caloric point of view, it doesn't matter to your body what the source of your calories is, although for good nutrition it is important to eat a balanced diet. And it doesn't matter on which day or days of the week you eat your calories. What matters is that you stay within your weekly salary.

Put another way, each day of the week that you eat minimally, you are depositing calories into your checking account. On Saturday and Sunday you withdraw these calories and safely spend them on your Wild Weekend splurge.

No-Think Diet

The best minds in the world of weight control have put together a no-think diet for you. Although calories do count, all the calories in all the foods you will eat and in all the meal plans in this book have been precounted for you.

Our experience told us that counting calories is not only dismal drudgery but also highly inaccurate. This probably doesn't astonish you, either. The Wild Weekend Diet assesses the calories for you, whether those calories are in a casserole dish or in a broiled steak. The assessment process gives you your best chance for success.

The calorie information is given to you in a very simple way. Each food has been assigned a unit value. You will add Wild Weekend Units (WWUs) as you choose and control the foods you eat on your Wild Weekend Diet.

Being Thin Forever

This is the diet you have been waiting for. It is more than a diet. It is a concept, and an information system by which you can regulate your weight healthfully and successfully for the rest of your life.

By using the principles and knowledge you acquire as you lose weight, you are also learning how to maintain that weight loss. As you experiment with and practice the principles of the Wild Weekend Diet you are at the same time mastering the system that will keep you thin forever.

Healthy Eating

Since we recommend the Wild Weekend Diet as a lifetime eating guide, you need to know how it relates to your body's nutritional needs.

Although each of our bodies has different requirements, there are common needs we share. These needs, Recommended Daily Allowances, have been established by the Food and Nutrition Board of the National Academy of Science.

Many people believe that these requirements are difficult to obtain from our nutrient-depleted soil, and, therefore, they take vitamins and minerals to supplement their food intake.

Although you will be eating healthfully, we, too, recommend food supplements in the form of good vitamin and mineral tablets. That is your second step to good health. The *first* step to good health is eating a well-balanced diet, and the Wild Weekend Diet is such a diet.

Well-Balanced Diet

It is essential to your body's good functioning that you eat daily amounts of protein, carbohydrates, and fats. A well-balanced diet includes these nutrients at each meal.

Protein is a body builder. It provides the amino acids necessary to produce cells for growth, maintenance, and repair of tissue. Amino acids are also necessary to produce enzymes and antibodies. Enzymes regulate your body processes. Antibodies fight infection and disease. On the Wild Weekend Diet you will be dining on protein when you eat fish, meat, poultry, cheese, and eggs.

The carbohydrates you eat give you energy and help you to think.

You will be eating carbohydrates at each meal when you eat bread, fruits, and vegetables.

Fats provide concentrated energy. They furnish protection for your body's organs and give your body insulation to keep you warm. The fats we recommend are primarily found in meat, eggs, cheese, and poultry.

CHAPTER 2

The Wild Weekend Diet

On the Wild Weekend Diet, as with all other eating plans, there are certain guidelines to follow. The Wild Weekend Diet works because you apportion your calories in a very unique way. You eat fewer calories during the week and spend those "saved" calories on the weekend when you want them the most. On the Wild Weekend Diet you enjoy your Saturday nights just the way you did in your pre-diet days. So, whether it's your birthday or a holiday, or just because you want a change, you will be eating along with the rest of your crowd even though you are on a weight-loss program.

Weekday Slimdown Plan and Wild Weekend Units

The Wild Weekend Diet is really two diets in one. The first diet is followed during the week, the second on the weekend.

The diet you follow Monday through Friday is called the Weekday Slimdown Plan (WSP). The WSP offers you a variety of menus to follow each weekday, each of which provides calories to bank away for weekend spending. The Weekday Slimdown Plan is a diet structured to guarantee your success. The structure dictates which food and how much you will eat at each meal.

You're probably interested in your weekend dining for the next several weekends and how the diet works. For starters, here is some information on Wild Weekend Units (WWUs).

Each of you has a Wild Weekend Unit allowance, which controls what and how much you eat during the Wild Weekend. Women are permitted a total of 36 WWUs and men get to eat 45. These WWUs are eaten exclusively on Saturday night and at Sunday brunch.

Women will eat 24 WWUs for dinner Saturday night and 12 WWUs for Sunday brunch. Men eat 31 WWUs Saturday night and 14 WWUs for Sunday brunch.

How Much Is a Wild Weekend Unit?

A Wild Weekend Unit averages no more than 75 calories. For instance, a food item that has been designated as 1 WWU may contain as few as 25 calories or it may contain as many as 75 calories. For you, though, it will always be 1 WWU.

How You'll Know How Many Units You're Eating

We have captured the most popular foods of the world and assigned WWUs to them. No matter if your favorite is an ethnic dish or a fast-food item, you'll probably find it on our list. And just in case it's not there, we'll show you how to create your own WWU lists.

For the present, rest assured that we have WWU values for Mexican, Greek, French, American, and Chinese as well as other cuisines.

What About the Other Weekend Meals?

We've chosen Saturday night and Sunday brunch as the stars of your eating week. You follow a prescribed eating plan for the other weekend meals. Saturday breakfast, Saturday lunch, and Sunday dinner find you making limited choices and eating slim.

We've Got a Little List

As you proceed through this book you'll discover your favorite foods and their WWU counts in Chapters 7, 8, and 9. These foods are arranged in logical patterns so that you'll be able to easily locate entrées and appetizers, grains and desserts. You won't have to commit these to memory; they will become part of your life as you continue to choose to lose.

You have the fun of making choices from those foods you like best. At a restaurant you may choose the seafood casserole or the rack of lamb or whatever is your pleasure. At a wedding you'll toast the bride and groom and eat the wedding cake, too. Even when you elect to entertain at home you'll be able to host a delicious meal that suits your taste and your Wild Weekend budget.

Coming Attractions

To give you an idea of just how much fun the Wild Weekend Diet can be, let me tell you about a meal Irene Z., who lost 12 pounds on the plan, chose recently while dining out at an Italian restaurant.

She started her evening off with a glass of Chianti. Red wine is her favorite choice no matter where or what she eats! She sipped her wine while munching the garlic bread, another favorite, and followed this with a first course of minestrone soup. By the time the entrée came, she decided to have a second glass of wine, which she drank while eating veal parmigiana, spaghetti with tomato sauce, and sautéed escarole with garlic. Irene chose tortoni for a sweet ending. All in all a very satisfying dinner.

Now let's see how that Italian dinner fit into her Saturday night allotment of 24 Wild Weekend Units:

	WILD WEEKEND UNITS
Chianti wine, 2 glasses	4
Minestrone soup, 1 cup	3

	WILD WEEKEND UNITS
Garlic bread, 1 piece	2
Veal parmigiana	7
Spaghetti with tomato sauce, 1 cup	3
Sautéed escarole	2
Tortoni	2
Espresso	0
	23

Just think, the Italian dinner of her dreams added up to just 23 WWUs. It's a dieter's heaven!

The Rest of the Weekend—No-Think Meals

Saturday breakfast finds you making a choice between 1 egg (poached or hard-boiled) or 1/4 cup of cottage cheese. You accompany your choice with 1 ounce of white or whole wheat bread and 1/2 grapefruit or 1/2 cup orange juice. Simple. Limited. Low in calories.

Saturday lunch you munch on lettuce and tomatoes with your choice of 3 ounces chicken or 3 ounces turkey breast. Add bread and fruit choices the same as you did for breakfast. Also add 1 cup skim milk. Simple. Limited. Low in calories.

Sunday dinner and the choosing is easy. You eat 6 ounces of plain, broiled or baked chicken or fish, and eat it with 1/2 cup of peas or a small potato. Eat all the salad you desire with low-calorie dressing and a piece of fruit, and 1 cup of skim milk. Simple. Limited. Low in calories.

Questions and Answers

Question: I have only 5 pounds to lose. Will this diet work for me?

Answer: Yes. No matter how little or how much weight you want to lose, the Wild Weekend Diet will show you how to do it and how to maintain your new figure.

Question: May I change the weekend meal plan around and use my Wild Weekend Units on Friday night instead of Saturday night?

Answer: Yes. You may use your WWUs on any night of the weekend. In this case switch the whole day. On Friday, eat the Saturday No-Think for breakfast, lunch, and dinner. On Saturday follow the Weekday Slimdown Plan.

Question: Is this diet safe for everyone?

Answer: The Wild Weekend Diet is healthy and nutritious. If, however, you have a medical condition, follow the directions of your physician; his or her advice always takes precedence.

Question: Do I have to eat breakfast? I'm just not hungry for breakfast.

Answer: You'll want to keep your energy level on an even keel for when you need it the most. For that reason we recommend that you eat a separate meal in the morning and one in the afternoon.

Question: This diet seems to go against everything I have ever read about losing weight. How can I lose weight if I eat lasagna and ice cream?

Answer: Food is neither bad nor good. All food does contain calories. As long as the total number of calories you eat weekly is less than the number your body needs to maintain your current weight, you will lose weight. You can eat those calories in whatever weekend foods you choose.

Question: Do I have to use all my Wild Weekend Units?

Answer: No. You can save calories and lose weight faster by not using them all.

Question: I'm a junk-food junkie. My dream is to give up dinner Saturday night and spend an entire evening munching out on junk foods. Will I lose weight if I do this?

Answer: Yes. As long as the foods you eat are within your total WWUs, munch away and have fun.

Question: I go to my mother's house to eat every weekend. How will I know how to count Wild Weekend Units?

Answer: As you become familiar with the various foods on the lists in

Chapters 7, 8, and 9, you will be able to make better and better judgments as to the number of WWUs that are contained in any particular food. When in doubt, count *high*.

Question: Is exercise necessary to lose weight on the Wild Weekend Diet?

Answer: The more you move, the more you'll lose, and faster, too. The more you lose, the better you'll feel. Exercise is also recommended for overall good health. However, it is not a requirement for weight loss.

CHAPTER 3

Off for the Weekend

So now it begins. As you embark on the exciting Wild Weekend way to slimness you know a lot about this journey already. You know you can eat any food in the world, and you know you're going to be able to diet and satisfy your taste for your favorite foods. You know you can go to your favorite restaurant and no longer feel guilty when you order. You know that you can—and should—take the weekend off from a rigid diet plan.

Balancing Your Budget

Let's go back for a minute to the idea of considering your Wild Weekend Units (WWUs) as your calorie salary. In the same way you budget your money to buy those things you need and want, so will you manage your WWU budget to have the food you want on the weekend.

Think for a minute about replenishing your wardrobe for the upcoming season. You know that you want a coat, suit, shoes, and a casual slacks outfit for lounging. And you know that each of these purchases must be made from the total sum of money you have budgeted and saved.

So, the scene is set. Your mission is to update your wardrobe. You know what you want to buy. And you know how much you have to spend. *Now* you still have to decide on how much to spend on *individual* items.

Probably your coat will cost the most. A coat can run anywhere from $79 to $500 or more. You have to decide how much of your clothing budget you want to spend on each item. After all, you're going to be wearing the clothes, so they have to suit your taste as well as your wallet. And all the time you're shopping you will have to bear in mind the money you have put aside for this project because you're committed to staying within that sum.

Choosing how you'll spend your WWUs is very similar to the above scenario. You can "buy" an entrée for 3 WWUs or you can "buy" an entrée for 8. *You* decide what to spend for your maximum satisfaction and enjoyment. Your budget is fixed by the Wild Weekend Diet. Remember, on Saturday night men are allotted 31 WWUs and women will choose 24 WWUs. For Sunday brunch men get to eat 15 WWUs and women 12.

Vive La Choice

You've worked for it, you deserve it, and now it's *yours*. Here are some guidelines on how you will exercise your freedom of choice.

Getting back to the above wardrobe shopping, we all know people who spend the major part of their budget on shoes. Open their closet doors, and the first thing you see is shoes . . . forty or fifty pairs. Believe me, it's not that rare.

Similarly there are people for whom dessert plays the starring role at dinner. To them everything that happens before the Baked Alaska finale is inconsequential compared to the end-of-the-meal event. So, if you are a dessert lover you'll want to think ahead and save more of your WWUs to spend at dessert time than someone whose food preference is a hefty entrée.

Staying with desserts for just a moment, you'll be happy to know that there are some relatively inexpensive treats. Jell-O is 2 WWUs, or you can choose 3 WWU desserts such as baked apple, ice cream, or a brownie. But if you are big on dessert, then enjoy and plan to spend 4 WWUs on cheesecake or chocolate mousse. It's diet okay, not to mention wonderful. Eat to your taste. As long as you stay within your WWU budget you're doing fine.

The Main Thing

Most people opt to spend most of their available WWUs on the dinner entrée. Three factors go into figuring the WWUs of these and other dishes. One is the *choice* of the main ingredient, another is the *portion size* of the main ingredient, and the third is the *method of preparation*.

Choice.

Portion size.

Method of preparation.

These are the components that determine the amount of WWUs any dish provides.

Choice

The main ingredient of an entrée is usually protein. The WWUs of fish, chicken, and beef and its different cuts vary greatly. Each of these proteins has a different "cost."

WWU assessments are made according to the number of calories each food provides. For example, 6 ounces of cooked flounder is assessed 2 WWUs, while 6 ounces of cooked swordfish counts as 3 WWUs. In the poultry area, 6 ounces of cooked chicken breast costs 4 WWUs, whereas 6 ounces of cooked goose adds 5 WWUs to your spending. The higher the fat content of beef, the higher the WWUs. For that reason the relatively lean eye-round roast beef costs one-third fewer WWUs than the same quantity of marbled prime rib.

Portion Size

WWU values also depend on "how much." We have assigned WWUs to foods based on lean methods of preparation and average-size portions of 6 ounces, cooked. To estimate the size of meat portions, look carefully at the diagrams that follow.

Roast Beef Round (lean only)

this thick

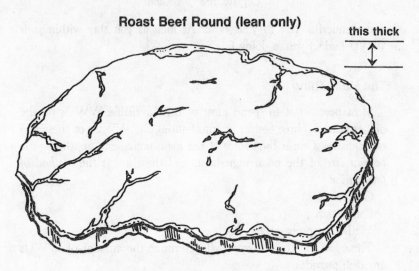

Two slices this size: 5 units

Ham (lean only)

this thick

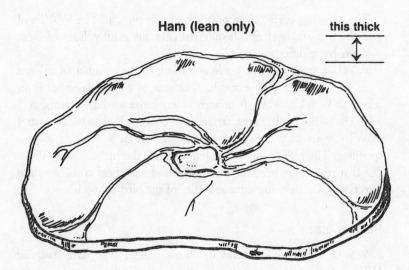

Two slices this size: 3 units

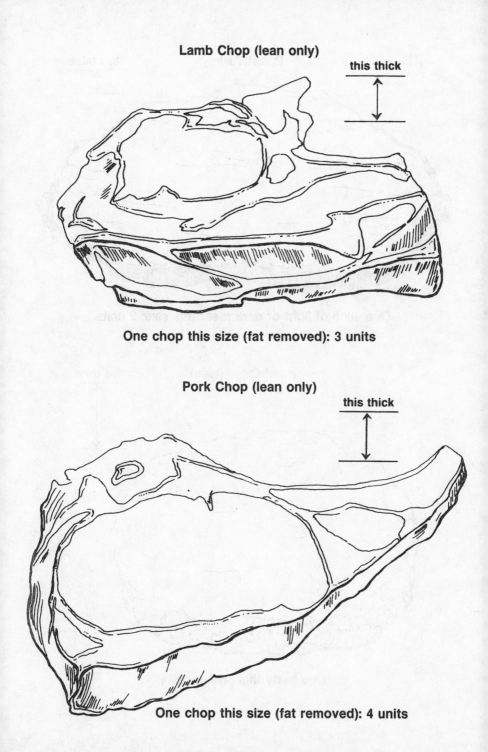

Lamb Chop (lean only)

this thick

One chop this size (fat removed): 3 units

Pork Chop (lean only)

this thick

One chop this size (fat removed): 4 units

Roast Turkey

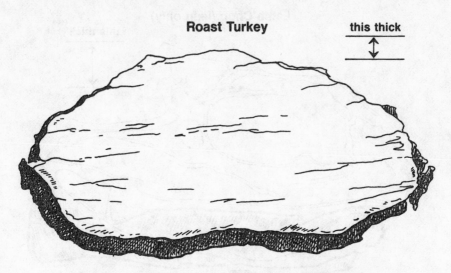

this thick

One slice of light or dark meat this size: 2 units

Hamburger (lean)

this thick

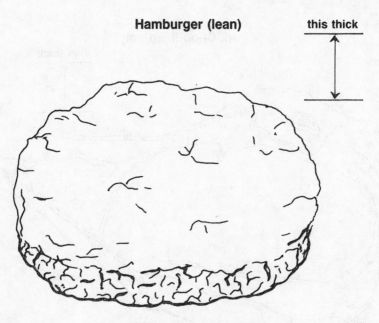

One patty this size: 4 units

Round Steak (lean only)

this thick

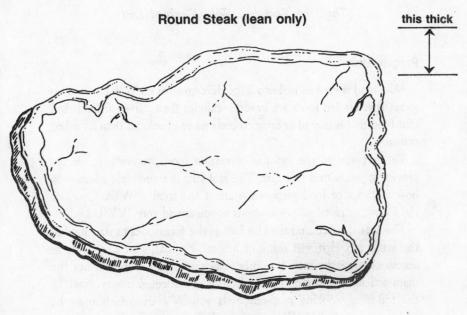

One piece this size: 4 units

Veal Cutlet (trimmed)

this thick

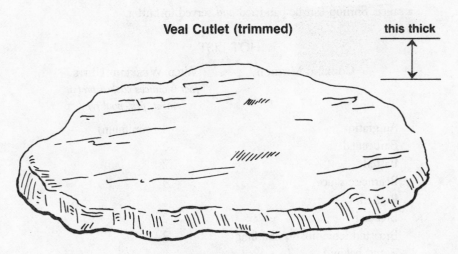

One cutlet this size: 2 units

Preparation

How food is cooked makes a large difference in its WWUs. It is no secret that broiled foods are lower in calories than pan-fried foods and that food that is coated or breaded costs more in calories than its naked cousin.

To alert you to the expense of certain food preparations, we are providing you with a Hot List. The Hot List is a complete guide as to how methods of food preparation affect the total WWUs. Consider the following Hot List preparations as you spend your WWU budget.

Think of the items on the Hot List as the accessories to your food in the same way that you think of a scarf, tie, hat, gloves, or hose as accessories to your basic wardrobe. Each accessory, although not the main article, must be purchased from your budgeted money. Each of the following cooking methods costs you WWUs, which must be added to the total WWUs of any dish. As you may choose to wear more than one accessory, so, too, may your dish have more than one Hot List item to be counted. Chicken may be breaded *and* served with a sauce. Shrimp can be pan-fried *and* served in butter.

HOT LIST

Cooking Method	Wild Weekend Units *(per 6 ounces cooked protein, meat, fish, poultry)*
Au gratin	4 (minimum)
Barbecued	2
Basted	2
Béarnaise sauce	4
Braised	2
Breaded	2
Broasted (combination broiling and baking)	2
Butter sauce	5

Buttery, buttered, served in butter	3
Cheesy, served with cheese	2
Cocktail sauce	2
Cooked in oil, made with oil	3
Creamed	4 (minimum)
Cream sauce	4
Crispy	3
Escalloped	4 (minimum)
Fried	3
Gravy	5
Hollandaise sauce	5
In a tomato base	2
In crust (fruit, dessert, etc.)	3
Pan-broiled	2
Pan-fried	3
Sautéed	3
Sour cream	2
Stewed	1 (minimum)
Stir-fry (no fat added)	1
Stuffed, bread or cracker crumbs	4 per fillet
style	3 per shrimp, clam, oyster, etc.
Sweet sauce	3
White sauce	3

If there is anything you don't understand on the menu, add 2 WWUs minimum.

The Cool Down

Now that we have "heated" you up with the Hot List, we'll stop a minute and "cool" you down with the Cool List. These are your best diet buddies. None of these methods add any extra WWUs to the base WWUs of the food item. Consider choosing these methods as you spend your Wild Weekend Units.

To carry the wardrobe metaphor one more step, the Cool List is a little like making your own clothes—the preparation is "free."

COOL LIST

Baked on a rack
Broiled
Charcoal-broiled
Dry-broiled (in lemon
    juice, bouillon, or with
    water)

Garden-fresh
Grilled
In its own juice (au jus)
In parchment paper
Poached
Roasted on rack
Steamed

Adding Up

So, how does all this work?

Let's start by looking at the many variations of cooking chicken and how those cooking methods affect the WWUs. A serving of chicken (6 ounces cooked, skinless, white meat) has a base WWU of 4. If you choose a preparation from the Cool List, you keep your WWUs to an economical 4. That means, if you eat it broiled, baked, poached, or steamed, or even charcoal-grilled, the WWUs remain at 4.

Let's say, though, that you're going to be adventurous and fry that little chicken. This is a Hot List method of preparation, and it increases your WWU count by 3, for a total of 7 WWUs for the same 6 ounces of chicken. Perhaps you elect to complete your eating adventure with some cream sauce over the chicken. Add another 4 WWUs for a total of *11 WWUs for the same amount of chicken.*

You really love chicken? Consider chicken cordon bleu. To tote up your WWUs you start again with the 4 for the plain, cooked chicken; add 2 WWUs for cheese; another 2 for ham; another 2 for breading; 3 for frying or baking in oil. And, of course, if you've topped it with a sauce or butter, you'll add 3 WWUs for every 2 tablespoons. If you've followed all this addition, you'll find yourself counting the chicken cordon bleu as 16 WWUs. Here it is shown another way:

	WWUS
6 ounces chicken breast	4
1½ ounces cheese	2
1½ ounces ham	2
breading*	2
frying*	3
white sauce*	3
	16

* All Hot List preparations are based on 6 ounces cooked protein.

What this tells you is that your adventure in eating an elaborately prepared entrée such as chicken cordon bleu will cost you 16 Wild and Wonderful Weekend Units.

You can never go wrong if you count on the high side. When you choose a portion size, the exact number of WWUs you don't know, add additional WWUs to preserve your weight-loss goals.

Let me give you a few more examples on how to figure what various preparations "cost."

Here's the beef and how some preparations of it affect its WWUs.

On your Wild Weekend eating spree, you may want to choose 12 ounces of cooked beef. This means you have to double the base WWUs of 8 WWUs assigned for 6 ounces of cooked beef to 16 WWUs.

If you eat it charcoal-broiled you begin and end with the 16 WWUs for 12 ounces. But if you pan-fry it as in steak au poivre, add 4 WWUs for the butter it is cooked in. Where did those 4 WWUs come from? Check the Hot List and you'll see pan-frying "costs" 2 WWUs for each 6 ounces of cooked protein. Since you doubled the portion, you must also double the WWU preparation cost.

You probably would not want more than 6 ounces of cooked beef bourguignon, so here you start counting with the base cost of 8 WWUs and add 5 for the gravy, for a total of 13 WWUs.

Fish is a dieter's buddy food. It is the lowest in calories of all proteins and, ounce for ounce, offers high food value for very little WWU cost.

However, fish, just like chicken and beef, can be rendered high in WWUs by certain cooking methods. Let's take 6 ounces of haddock or any white-type fish. The base WWU for 6 ounces of haddock is 3. You can eat it broiled, baked, poached, or steamed, and its WWU remains at 3.

Fish cooked in the above manner can be delicious, especially if not overcooked. But what if you love fried fish? Then choose a Hot List method and increase the WWUs by 3 for a total of 6 for the same piece of fish. And if tartar sauce is a favorite part of your fried fish, add another 3 WWUs for a total of 9.

Fish can be prepared in infinite variety. For the gourmet dish Sole Véronique, start with the base WWUs of 3. Add 3 for the sauté preparation and then add 5 units for the butter sauce it "swims" in and an additional WWU for the white grapes in the sauce. You now have a total of 12 WWUs for Sole Véronique.

Let's look at Sole Véronique in more detail:

	WWUS
6 ounces sole	3
sautéed in butter	3*
butter sauce	5*
	11

* Hot List preparation "cost" for 6 ounces of protein.

Baked Stuffed

When you sit down to eat fish, you may automatically assume that you're sitting down to a low-calorie dish. That's not necessarily true, dear innocents. We know of a recipe for baked stuffed jumbo shrimp (four pieces) that has a WWU value of 17. True, the "naked" shrimp has a WWU value of only 2. So what could happen in a shrimp's life to boost the WWUs so high? Baked stuffed is what!

The creator of this recipe, a well-known restaurateur in Massachusetts, makes a cracker-crumb stuffing using 1 cup crumbs (7 WWUs), water, spices, seasonings, and 5½ tablespoons of butter, bringing the total WWUs for four baked stuffed jumbo shrimp to 17! Each shrimp is equal to more than 4 Wild Weekend Units!

Whenever you see the words *baked stuffed* or *en casserole,* you need to add 4 WWUs per 6-ounce cooked protein fillet (fish, poultry) or 3 WWUs *per* shrimp, clam, crab leg or claw, lobster tail, oyster, etc., to the basic WWUs for that protein.

Remember, for dieters ignorance may be momentary bliss, but its consequence is often long-term disaster.

Questions to Consider

Enjoy making your food choices on the Wild Weekend Diet! This is a unique approach to weight loss, and you will be successful as long as you take some time with it. *But you are not relieved of taking responsibility for the foods you eat.* Although you will find WWUs for many foods in this book, they are only reliable estimates based on standard, accepted recipes, and variations in foods and food preparation do occur. You have the choice of the world, but use your head. As you eat a food bring into action all of your senses (sight, smell, touch, sound, and taste) to help you more accurately assess the WWUs of a food. Ask yourself these questions:

- Is there more here than the standard WWU portion size?
- Does this food taste especially oily, buttery, or greasy?
- Does this food taste unusually sweet?
- Does this food feel greasy in my mouth? This is particularly important if you've ordered a food prepared without oil or butter.
- Is the word *smothered* used in describing the food?
- Does this food smell or taste differently than it should? Is there a hint of frying or sautéing?
- Is this food garnished with items not included in your total WWUs?
- Is there heavy marbling in a beef or poultry serving?
- Is there a greasy residue left on your plate?

For every *yes* answer to the above questions add at least 2 WWUs to the WWU total of that entrée.

You'll never go wrong if you count too high. You'll only lose weight a little faster!

Night Life

Whether you're home or abroad, in a restaurant or attending a wedding or other social event, your time of decision has arrived. It is Saturday night on your Wild Weekend Diet. The only thing that stands between you and what you eat is your decision. Let's try out the system.

Logically we begin at the beginning. You'll find that appetizers and soups range from a low of 1 WWU to a high of 7 WWUs. Bear this in mind as you think ahead to the meal to come.

Even moderate drinkers find Saturday night a time to enjoy one or two drinks and perhaps some wine. Cocktail WWUs range from 2 to 4 per glass. Say you choose to drink 2 martinis ahead of the meal, 4 WWUs. Now let's choose an appetizer that has a relatively low WWU value and start our meal with fruit cocktail and a small scoop of sherbet at 2 WWUs.

So far, your bill totals 6 WWUs. Now let's talk about the rest of the meal. Most Saturday night meals contain at least four different foods— salad, entrée, starch, and vegetable—so let's adopt that pattern.

Let's decide on a garden salad with 2 tablespoons bleu cheese dressing for 4 WWUs, recognizing that we could have chosen a small, dry garden-style salad for no WWUs or a Greek salad with a generous serving of feta cheese and olive oil-type dressing for 8 WWUs.

Our entrée will be veal scallopini at 5 WWUs, baked potato with 3 tablespoons of sour cream for 3 WWUs, and string beans, which have no WWU cost. Two glasses of wine will accompany this dish nicely.

Now we'll go back and total the WWUs before we choose dessert.

		WWUs
Cocktails/wine	2 martinis	4
	2 glasses white wine	4

Appetizer	Fruit cocktail with sherbet	2
Salad	Garden salad with 2 tablespoons bleu cheese dressing	4
Entrée	Veal scallopini (6 ounces)	5
Starch	Baked potato with 3 tablespoons sour cream	3
Vegetable	String beans (no butter)	0
		22

You've now spent 22 WWUs, and if you're a woman, you have 2 WWUs to spend on dessert, coffee or tea, or an after-dinner drink; if you are a man, you have 9 more WWUs to spend.

You might select peach cobbler for 2 WWUs, accompanied by black coffee or tea for no additional WWUs, or perhaps you'll choose brandy or a liqueur for 1 WWU and a light dessert such as ice milk for 1 WWU.

A word of caution. Coffee and tea are not always WWU-free. If you like sweetened, lightened coffee or tea, you need to add 1 WWU each time you add sugar and cream or milk to your beverage.

Now let's add up how many WWUs we spent this evening:

		WWUS
Cocktails/wine	2 martinis	4
	2 glasses white wine	4
Appetizer	Fruit cocktail with sherbet	2
Salad	Garden salad with 2 tablespoons bleu cheese dressing	4
Entrée	Veal scallopini	5
Starch	Baked potato with 3 tablespoons sour cream	3

Vegetable	String beans (no butter)	0
Dessert	Peach cobbler	2
Beverage	Tea and lemon	0
		24

A wonderful meal, and if you're a woman, you're right on the mark; if you're a man, you've come in under your Wild Weekend Saturday night budget by 7 WWUs and are getting thinner faster.

Next Weekend

This Saturday night we had dinner together. Next week you're on your own. By the time you finish this book you will know how *you* want to spend your Wild Weekend Units. You will know everything you need to know before you enjoy your meal because you will find all the WWU information in Chapters 7, 8, and 9. Spend some time now to browse through these chapters, as you would a mail-order catalog, so that by the time you are ready to spend WWUs you will have an idea of how to fit the foods you love into your WWU budget. Have fun, and *bon appétit!*

CHAPTER 4

Weekday Slimdown Plan

Smile

The Wild Weekend is coming!

At first glance the Weekday Slimdown Plan (WSP) looks much like other low-calorie diets, but it isn't. The difference lies in the role that the WSP plays in the Wild Weekend Diet.

The WSP is the heart of the Wild Weekend Diet. It is a no-choice, carefully planned, and satisfying diet. Its structure provides the support you need for weight-loss success.

The operative word here is *control*. Controlled eating equals controlled calories, and controlled calories equal weight loss and weight control.

Monday through Friday, you set your alarm clock. When it rings, you don't think about it, you get up. Same with the WSP. Don't think about it during the week, just do it! Because when the weekend comes, you've got a lovely morning sleep to look forward to, and even lovelier WWUs to spend.

Fat Burn-Up Time

The Weekday Slimdown Plan provides 4,000 calories a week for women and 5,200 calories for men. All of these calories are consumed from Monday through Friday. During this time women will be eating only about 800 calories per day and men will be eating 1,040, which is far less energy than your body needs to operate. This is the time, therefore, when your body will be burning up the energy you've stored away as fat.

If you and the Wild Weekend Diet are to work together as a successful partnership, you must adhere strictly to guidelines. You cannot allow yourself any additions or exchanges that might in some way interfere with your weight loss. Adding extra food or beverages to the WSP will slow your weight loss down considerably.

Enjoy your control in the same way you enjoy a more structured lifestyle during the week. And all the while you are following the WSP, enjoy thinking that this is the time you are burning up those unwanted pounds and inches.

Temptations

Well-meaning friends, television commercials, newspaper and magazine ads, supermarket strategy, co-workers, family, etc., will each, at some time, give you permission to go off the diet and will always create detours and roadblocks on your road to success. Depend on it. You are going to face temptations every step of the way. That's life. But, forewarned is forearmed. Stand up to these temptations and remind yourself that the weekend is coming.

As a matter of fact, be one step ahead. The best defense against anyone or anything's offense is your own resolve. Put yourself in charge of your eating and your weight loss. Taking care of your responsibilities is your best protection against miseating.

Another kind of temptation is the one that beckons you to skip a meal here or a part of a meal there. This habit will erode the most fervent goals. It is well known that breakfast skippers experience a strong late-afternoon food urge, as well as an energy lag. And that's only part of the problem that comes from meal skipping. More insidious is that feeling of entitlement the skipper gets that allows her/him to have that "little something" in exchange for the foods s/he's given up. That "little something" rarely takes the form of RyKrisp or a carrot stick.

WSP Strategy

As with any plan of action, any worthy objective, there must be a strategy. A goal is the overview. With the goal firmly in sight, strategy defines the method used to reach the goal. The strategy for the WSP is *getting ready*, by psyching yourself up, *getting set*, by arranging your life so that you can diet well, and *go*, with the plans we provide.

Getting Ready

The best time to begin this step is, of course, right now. From this minute on think of yourself as ready to start your most exciting diet, a diet that is so well fashioned around your needs and wants that you are a truly clever person for having arranged things so well.

Keep getting ready by telling yourself each day that you will succeed on the Wild Weekend Diet. Why wouldn't you? And, while you're at it, tell yourself that this is it; this is your last diet. Also let yourself know all the way inside you that you are a winner and that you can do the things you want to do. And what you want to do now is to get thin!

Close your eyes right now and picture yourself as a thin person . . . more attractive, more self-confident, healthier, doing the things you want to do, looking the way you want to look, having more energy. Bring this picture back to your mind every single day as soon as you wake up and again just before you go to sleep, and anytime during the day when you may doubt your ability to succeed. If you can dream it and keep that dream in front of you, you will succeed.

Think of losing weight as your *right*. You, too, have the right to be healthier. And to have a more exciting life-style. Keep telling yourself this. This is your last diet. Believe it.

Getting Set

There are two parts to getting started: one is getting rid of the things you don't want in the house; the second is to get the food and equipment you need to follow the WSP.

Each of us finds certain foods and/or situations hard to handle when we're dieting.

Some people succumb to the smell of freshly baked brownies. Others have trouble getting the batter into the oven. Still others find food a comfort when anxiety is high before a big meeting, or as a friend when no one else is around. Some people let themselves get so hungry that they eat before they even sit down at the table. For some of us, eating with friends gives us permission to eat as they eat. Only you know what your pitfalls are. Think ahead to those foods and situations that have to be handled now. Don't think about what your family needs to eat, think in terms of what you can't handle around the house. Don't promise yourself to be strong. You don't need to be a tower of strength, you need to be successful at weight loss.

As far as hard-to-handle situations are concerned, think about what you can do to make them go better. By all means ask for the help of those involved. Together you can brainstorm new ideas on controlling those difficulties we all have. Plan now. Failing to plan is planning to fail. You owe it to yourself to put some time in on this project.

Go shopping and spend what you must to have the foods and tools at hand that will get you through. Personalize the two lists.

Weight Control Tools

- Postage scale: To weigh meats, fish, poultry, cheese, and bread.
- Measuring cups: To measure vegetables, fruits, and cottage cheese.
- Measuring spoons: To measure diet salad dressing, diet jelly, and extracts.
- Food diary: To use daily to plan your menu or to keep a record

of what you are eating. This is an excellent eating behavior to adopt.
- Shopping list: To use weekly to be sure you always have the WSP foods on hand.

Shopping List for WSP

Artificial sweetener
Bean sprouts
Bouillon (cubes or powder)
 Beef
 Chicken
 Onion
 Vegetable
Breads
 English muffins
 Melba toast
 Pocket breads, small
 Pumpernickel
 Rye
 Whole wheat
Cereals (unsweetened)
 Oatmeal, plain
 Puffed flakes
Cheese
 Cottage, low-fat
 Parmesan, grated
Consommé
Eggs, medium
Extracts
 Brandy
 Butter
 Vanilla
Fruit (apples, berries,

cantaloupe, oranges,
 peaches, plums)
Dietetic
In its own juice (pineapple)
Juice (grapefruit, lemon,
 lime)
Water-packed
Herbs and spices
 Bay leaves
 Cinnamon
 Curry powder
 Dill
 Garlic
 Ginger
 Nutmeg
 Onion flakes
 Oregano
 Pepper
 Rosemary
 Salt
Horseradish
Jellies, dietetic
Leafy greens
 Collard greens
 Lettuce
 Mustard greens
 Spinach

Maple syrup, dietetic
Meats, fish, poultry
  Chicken
  Fish (fresh white-type,
    shellfish)
  Fish, canned (water-packed)
  Liver, any kind
  Turkey breast (deli counter),
    roast
  Veal
Milk
  Buttermilk
  Non-fat dry

  Skim
Pan spray, non-stick
Salad dressing, dietetic
Soda, diet
Soy sauce
Tabasco sauce
Teriyaki sauce
Tofu
Tomato juice
Vegetables of your choice
  (fresh, frozen, or canned)
Vinegar
Worcestershire sauce

Now get out a piece of paper and make a shopping list. Go through your cabinets and refrigerator and write down what you need. You must have all the foods in your home ahead of time so you will not be faced with the dilemma of what to eat. The WSP menus let you know exactly what you will be eating.

Go

It's time to begin. Start today on the Weekday Slimdown Plan #1. *Diet through the first weekend following the Weekday Slimdown Plan with no Wild Weekend.* This is very important.

- You put yourself in a diet frame of mind.
- You remove yourself from anytime, anywhere, and any-old-thing eating.

Here are the WSP guidelines you will follow. Do they sound familiar? That's because it is well known that they are correct for people who want to get thin.

1. Broil, bake, boil, steam, grill, charcoal, or poach all meats, fish, and poultry.
2. Remove all visible fat before cooking.

3. Remove all poultry and fish skin before eating. Before cooking is preferable.
4. Use no added fats or oils in cooking or food preparation; e.g., mayonnaise, butter, etc.
5. Weigh all meats, fish, poultry, *after* cooking to be sure you are eating the correct amount.*
6. Weigh all breads and hard cheese.
7. Measure the fruits and vegetables and cottage cheese that specify amounts.
8. Use a nonstick pan spray (minimum amount) to fry or scramble your eggs.

WEEKLY MEAL PATTERN

Sunday	Monday	Tuesday	Wednesday	Thursday	Friday	Saturday
Wild Weekend Brunch	Weekday Slimdown Plan WSP	Weekday Slimdown Plan WSP	Weekday Slimdown Plan WSP	Weekday Slimdown Plan WSP	Weekday Slimdown Plan WSP	Saturday Breakfast
						Saturday Lunch
Sunday Dinner						**Wild Weekend** Dinner

Delicious Eating on the WSP

Eating on the WSP need not be bland and boring. There are many ways you can add zest and zip to low-calorie meals. We have taken out the calories, and now we'll show you how to add flavor and appeal.

* NOTE: One pound of raw meat, fish, or skinless, boneless chicken yields 12 ounces cooked meat; one half pound raw equals 6 ounces cooked meat, fish, or poultry.
One pound of raw chicken with skin and bone yields 10 ounces cooked.

	DAY 1	DAY 2	DAY 3	DAY 4	DAY 5
BREAKFAST	1 egg, medium 1 ounce bread 1 orange, small	1/4 cup cottage cheese 1 ounce bread 1/2 cup pineapple chunks, packed in own juice	1 ounce low-fat cheese 1/2 English muffin 1 cup tomato juice	1/4 cup cottage cheese 1/2 cup cooked oatmeal 1/2 cup orange juice	1 egg, medium 1 ounce bread 1/2 cup grapefruit juice
LUNCH	3/4 cup cottage cheese 1 ounce bread	3 ounces turkey breast* 6 pieces Melba toast	3 ounces tuna, water-packed 1 ounce bread	3 ounces soft tofu or 3 ounces canned shellfish 1 ounce bread	3 ounces chicken breast* 1/2 English muffin
DINNER	4 ounces white-type fish* 1/2 cup peas	4 ounces liver* 1/2 cup onions	4 ounces chicken* 1/2 cup beets	4 ounces veal* 1/2 cup corn	4 ounces turkey breast* 1/2 cup winter squash

*Weights for meat, fish, and poultry are cooked weights.

As Desired: Bean sprouts, broccoli, carrots, celery, cucumber, green pepper, lettuce, mushrooms, spinach, string beans, and tomato for lunch and dinner.

Extras: Artificial sweetener, bouillon, coffee, diet beverages, 1 tablespoon diet salad dressing (per day), 2 teaspoons dietetic jelly (per day), extracts, herbs, lemon, lime, mustard, pepper, salt, tea, vinegar, water, spices, Worcestershire sauce.

Every Day Snack: 8 ounces skim milk or buttermilk *and* 1 small apple, peach, plum, orange, or 1/2 cup berries, 1/4 cantaloupe, 1/2 grapefruit, or 1/2 cup fruit packed in water or own juice, or 1/2 cup orange or grapefruit juice.

For Men Only: Add daily 2 ounces bread *and* 3 ounces cooked meat, fish, or poultry.

ANY WHOLE DAY MAY BE EXCHANGED FOR ANY OTHER WHOLE DAY.

Flavor Tips

How many tablespoons of butter per week do you need to give up to lose a pound of fat? Only thirty-five, and most people easily consume that amount in six or seven days. Losing a pound a week is worth giving up butter, don't you think? But you don't have to give up the taste of butter. You can use it by the bottle (butter-flavored extract) or sprinkle it on foods to your heart's content (butter-flavored powder).

You may not be able to poach your fish in wine on the WSP or spark up a sizzling flaming steak with brandy, but you can add the flavor to your meals by using rum, brandy, or sherry extract.

Here are some more flavorful suggestions:

- Use a nonstick pan spray for frying eggs, fish, and skinless chicken.
- Sauté vegetables in one tablespoon of water with one bouillon cube or one tablespoon of bouillon, powdered.
- Shake a small amount of grated Parmesan cheese on steamed vegetables or broiled fish.
- Marinate vegetables, fish, or chicken in diet salad dressing for a treat.
- Use flavored vinegars for variety on salads.
- Become a spice-and-herb connoisseur and experiment with different combinations on vegetables and meats.
- Use lemon juice by the bottle. Wonderful on vegetables.
- Dab a little soy or teriyaki sauce on fish or chicken for an Oriental flair.

De-lite-ful Recipes for You

Be creative as you prepare your WSP meals. To get you started here are some delicious recipes for you to use. Each recipe follows the guidelines for the WSP.

BREAKFAST RECIPES

(All breakfast recipes serve one)

A Breakfast for People Who Don't Like Breakfast

1/4 cup cottage cheese
     cinnamon to taste
     artificial sweetener to taste
2   slices very thin bread

Mix cheese, cinnamon, and sweetener together. Spread on toast and bake in oven at 325° for 6–7 minutes. Serves 1.

Sunny Eggs

1   1-ounce pocket bread, split and toasted
1   teaspoon prepared mustard
     tarragon
1   egg
     salt and pepper to taste

Spread pocket halves with mustard and sprinkle with tarragon. Place in a pan sprayed with nonstick coating. Break an egg over one pocket half and sprinkle with salt and pepper. Broil 6 inches from heat source for 4–5 minutes or until egg is set. If desired, garnish with parsley. Top with remaining half of pocket bread.

Pancakes

1   ounce white bread
1/2 cup skim milk
1   egg
1/2 teaspoon vanilla
2   packets artificial sweetener
     nonstick pan spray

Blend together all ingredients and "fry" in sprayed skillet.
Serve with dietetic maple syrup. Serves 1.

VARIATIONS:
Use buttermilk in place of skim milk.
Spread with dietetic jelly and roll up like a crepe.

LUNCH RECIPES

(All lunch recipes serve one.)

Tuna Sandwich on Toast

11/2 ounces canned tuna, drained, water-packed
1/4   cup cottage cheese
1   teaspoon horseradish
1   tablespoon Thousand Island diet dressing
      thick wedge of lettuce
2   slices very thin bread, toasted

Mix tuna, cottage cheese, dressing, and horseradish together, and spread on toast. Top with lettuce for a mile-
high sandwich.

Chicken Salad

3   ounces cooked chicken, diced
1/4 cup celery, sliced diagonally
1   tablespoon French diet dressing
     dash of pepper
2   teaspoons lemon juice

Toss all ingredients together and serve. Good with tuna, too.

10-Minute Luncheon Special

1   1-pound can Chinese vegetables
1   4-ounce can mushrooms, drained
3   ounces cooked chicken or 3 ounces
     canned shrimp
1/4 teaspoon garlic powder
1   packet artificial sweetener
3   tablespoons soy sauce

Mix all ingredients together. Simmer about 10 minutes.

Minced Clam Lunch

2   packets instant chicken or vegetable bouillon
1   3-ounce can minced clams
1   can bean sprouts, drained
1   4-ounce can mushrooms (optional)

Heat bouillon with clams in their liquid. Add bean sprouts and mushrooms, if desired.

Spring Chicken Salad

1/2	cucumber, very thinly sliced
1/2	head romaine lettuce, torn in pieces
2	stalks celery, chopped
3	ounces cooked chicken, diced
3	tablespoons tarragon vinegar
1/2	teaspoon dry mustard
2	drops Worcestershire sauce
	freshly ground pepper

Combine cucumber, romaine lettuce, celery, and chicken. Mix together vinegar, mustard, Worcestershire sauce, and pepper. Pour over chicken salad and mix well.

DINNER RECIPES

Baked Fish

1	cup skim milk
1	teaspoon dill
1	teaspoon parsley
1	pound fish fillet (haddock, flounder, or other white-type fish)
	pinch of dry mustard
1/4	cup green peppers, minced
2	celery stalks, diced

Mix all ingredients together and pour over fish. Bake for 25 minutes at 350°. Serves 3.

Fish or Chicken Cutlets

Marinate any white-type fish or chicken for two hours in one of the following and broil:

1/4 cup lemon juice mixed with 1/4 cup chopped parsley and onion powder

1/2 cup skim milk; sprinkle with Parmesan cheese before broiling

1/2 cup buttermilk; add capers and/or oregano before broiling

1/4 cup lemon or lime juice mixed with 1/4 cup soy sauce

Sukiyaki

4	ounces cooked chicken or 4 ounces cooked turkey
1	medium onion, sliced
1/4	cup mushrooms, sliced
1/4	pound fresh spinach, torn in pieces
1	packet artificial sweetener
1/4	cup celery, sliced
1	packet instant beef or vegetable bouillon
2	scallions, sliced lengthwise
1/2	cup water
	soy sauce

Mix all ingredients together in saucepan. Bring to a boil and simmer until celery is barely tender, or about 7 minutes. Do not overcook. Serves 1.

Company Chicken

1   cup orange juice
1/4 cup lemon juice
1   packet artificial sweetener
1   teaspoon marjoram
1   pound cooked chicken, boned and sliced
1   tablespoon chopped parsley

Combine juices and artificial sweetener. Add marjoram. Cook over low heat for 5 minutes, stirring constantly. Place chicken in casserole, spoon sauce over it, and bake for 15 minutes at 350°. Garnish with parsley when ready to serve. Serves 6.

Broiled Chicken

2   2½- to 3-pound chickens, quartered
     lemon juice
     celery strips
1/2 cup soy sauce
1/2 cup tarragon vinegar
1/2 cup water

Brush chickens with lemon juice and cover with celery strips. Marinate 1 hour in remaining ingredients. Broil on each side about 20 minutes or until tender, basting occasionally with marinade. Weigh chicken portion without skin or bones. Serves 6–8.

Chicken in a Crock Pot

Basic Recipe:

- 4 chicken breasts, without skin
- 4 cups of any mix of celery, broccoli, and green pepper
- 2 cups of any mix of tomatoes, carrots, and onions

Put all vegetables into crock pot and place chicken over them. Pour sauce over all, cover, and cook 6–8 hours on low setting. Serves 4.

SAUCE 1: salt, pepper, rosemary leaves, 1 cup wine vinegar, 1 cup water

SAUCE 2: salt, pepper, paprika, garlic powder, 1 teaspoon oregano, 3 tablespoons lemon juice, 1 cup water.

Baked Italian Chicken

- 6 chicken breasts, halved, with skin removed
  salt and pepper to taste
- 1 teaspoon rosemary leaves
- 1/2 cup wine vinegar
- 1/2 cup water

Place chicken in baking dish. Combine remaining ingredients and pour over chicken in baking dish. Bake at 350° for 1 hour.

NOTE: Turkey may be substituted in any of the chicken recipes.

Chicken Livers

1   pound chicken livers
1/2   packet artificial sweetener
1/2   cup celery, sliced
2   cups tomato juice
1   teaspoon vinegar

Combine all ingredients and simmer until celery and livers are tender. Serves 3.

Curry of Veal

1 1/2   pounds veal, cut up
1   orange, peeled and cut up
2   packets instant beef, chicken, or vegetable bouillon
1/4   teaspoon ginger
1/2   packet artificial sweetener
1/2   teaspoon curry powder
1 1/2   cups water

Brown veal in heavy skillet. Add remaining ingredients and cook on low fire until veal is tender. Add water if needed. Serves 4.

Veal and Pepper Stew

6   ounces veal, cut in chunks
1   packet instant vegetable or chicken bouillon
3/4   cup water
    paprika and garlic to taste
1   tomato, diced
1   green pepper
1   tablespoon onion flakes

Heat water with bouillon. Brown veal in bouillon, remove meat, and set aside. Sauté onion flakes and pepper in bouillon, and season with paprika and garlic. Add tomato and veal. Cover and simmer for one hour or until veal is done. Serves 1.

Sweet-and-Sour Veal

1½	pounds ground veal
2	tablespoons Worcestershire sauce
1	tablespoon prepared yellow mustard
1	tablespoon soy sauce
4	orange slices
1	large or 2 small green peppers, cut into strips
1	packet instant vegetable, chicken, or beef bouillon
3/4	cup water
1	13½-ounce can unsweetened pineapple chunks
	bean sprouts

Combine ground veal with Worcestershire sauce, mustard, and soy sauce. Mix thoroughly. Shape into 12 balls. Heat water, add bouillon, sauté meatballs in bouillon, and add remaining ingredients. Simmer for 20–30 minutes or until done. Place veal balls on hot bean sprouts and pour sauce over all. Serves 4.

Hunger

You may experience some hunger on the WSP. This is quite natural.

Hunger is the signal that your body is running on a calorie deficit and is therefore burning up your extra body fat to obtain needed energy. What you are feeling here is yourself losing weight. Think of it that way and turn it into a good feeling.

True hunger pangs last for only twenty minutes. If you distract yourself for this amount of time, your hunger will be gone and you will be comfortable again.

Have courage. Each time you experience hunger and decide to respond by not eating, you are training your body to learn new responses. Nobody has ever starved to death in twenty minutes. Hunger does not mean you have to eat. Here's what you can do instead of eating when hunger pangs strike. See what you can add to this list:

- Take a brisk walk in the fresh air.
- Exercise your green thumb—prune, root, water, and feed your plants.
- Prepare a large goblet of water, ice, and a twist of lemon. Sip slowly with a straw.
- Play with children and/or pets (yours or somebody else's).
- Enjoy a long, hot bath with bath oil or bubbles for an extra treat.
- Write a letter to a friend.
- Run up and down your stairs until you need to rest.
- Call a dieting friend or a positive-thinking one.
- Gargle with mouthwash.
- Make a list of nice, pleasant, happy things in your life.
- Pray.
- Knit, crochet, or sew small projects, so you can enjoy the satisfaction of finishing them.
- Buy a magazine, curl up, and enjoy it from cover to cover.
- Reach for your mate instead of your plate.
- Relax with a soothing warm drink.
- Talk on the phone with a friend (use any extension but the one in the kitchen).
- Brush your teeth.
- Make a list of things you can accomplish in five minutes (you'll be amazed at how many there are), and then do them. Cross each one out as you finish it.
- Open your back door and scream.

- Polish your nails.
- Go shopping and treat yourself to something fun (facial), luxurious (perfume), pretty (scarf), or extra (fancy writing paper).
- Shovel snow, plant bulbs or seeds, mow grass, rake leaves.
- Take your dog for a walk.
- Put on a record and dance.
- Read a book.
- Go swimming.
- Cry.
- Kick a pillow around the house.
- Add chocolate-flavored skim milk powder in teaspoon amounts to coffee.
- Think thin.
- Exercise.
- When all else fails, look in a three-way mirror.

What Weight?

This sounds like such a simple question. However, many people are never quite sure what they should weigh.

They may find out that a person whose figure they admire weighs 130 pounds, for example, and then they figure that's how much they should weigh. Or some people may read in a magazine or newspaper that if your height is *x*, then you should weigh *y*. These two examples certainly provide some guidelines, but are they right for *you?*

As with many other important questions we encounter in life for which we would like neat black-and-white answers, all we can offer is a range of gray—there is no number we can give you that is exactly right for you.

What follows are the newest Metropolitan Life Insurance Company Height and Weight Tables. These tables are based on the 1979 Build Study, Society of Actuaries and Association of Life Insurance Medical Directors of America, 1980. The following weights include wearing indoor clothing, and also include women wearing shoes with 1-inch heels.

1983 METROPOLITAN HEIGHT & WEIGHT TABLES
WOMEN

| Height | | Small | Medium | Large |
Feet	Inches	Frame	Frame	Frame
4	10	102–111	109–121	118–131
4	11	103–113	111–123	120–134
5	0	104–115	113–126	122–137
5	1	106–118	115–129	125–140
5	2	108–121	118–132	128–143
5	3	111–124	121–135	131–147
5	4	114–127	124–138	134–151
5	5	117–130	127–141	137–155
5	6	120–133	130–144	140–159
5	7	123–136	133–147	143–163
5	8	126–139	136–150	146–167
5	9	129–142	139–153	149–170
5	10	132–145	142–156	152–173
5	11	135–148	145–159	155–176
6	0	138–151	148–162	158–179

MEN

| Height | | Small | Medium | Large |
Feet	Inches	Frame	Frame	Frame
5	2	128–134	131–141	138–150
5	3	130–136	133–143	140–153
5	4	132–138	135–145	142–156
5	5	134–140	137–148	144–160
5	6	136–142	139–151	146–164
5	7	138–145	142–154	149–168
5	8	140–148	145–157	152–172
5	9	142–151	148–160	155–176
5	10	144–154	151–163	158–180
5	11	146–157	154–166	161–184
6	0	149–160	157–170	164–188
6	1	152–164	160–174	168–192
6	2	155–168	164–178	172–197
6	3	158–172	167–182	176–202
6	4	162–176	171–187	181–207

What is good about the Metropolitan tables is that you can choose from a broad choice of "what's right" according to the actuarial criterion of how long people live. What that means is that people live longer at these weights.

The following is what The Diet Workshop recommends to its members. These charts were created by Norman Joliffe, M.D., the New York doctor who created the idea of losing weight by eating a balanced diet. These charts assume both men and women are wearing indoor clothing but *no* shoes.

You may not want to be the weight indicated on any table or chart. It's your choice. Be the weight you want to be. Be the weight that feels best for you. Not everyone is meant to be a Twiggy. You'll be at your ideal weight when you can look in the mirror, turn yourself all the way around, and smile and say "you look great," or even, "I can live with this!"

Goals

All that said and done, it's important to set that goal *now* so that when you get there, you'll know that you've arrived! So, before you even start the Wild Weekend Diet, decide what you want to weigh. Think back to when you looked and felt your best. Even if that was twenty years ago, you can weigh that weight, feel that good again.

Nothing wrong with interim goals either. Some people feel motivated best by short-term goals. If you want to lose ten pounds before you determine just what your long-term weight will be, that's okay, too.

The idea is to set a goal, be it your final number or a definite number of pounds. Choose what feels best to you. But *choose*. And just so you won't forget your goal, write it down on the title page of this book. NOW.

Goal Range

I created the principle of Goal Range to deal with the maddening imprecision of the weight-loss process, to lessen the frustration of look-

THE DIET WORKSHOP® WEIGHT CHART
WOMEN

| Height | | Small | Medium | Large |
Feet	Inches	Frame	Frame	Frame
4	10	108	116	124
4	11	110	118	126
5	0	113	121	129
5	1	116	124	132
5	2	120	128	136
5	3	123	132	140
5	4	127	136	144
5	5	130	139	148
5	6	134	142	152
5	7	138	146	156
5	8	142	150	160
5	9	146	154	163
5	10	150	158	166
5	11	154	162	170
6	0	158	166	174

MEN

| Height | | Small | Medium | Large |
Feet	Inches	Frame	Frame	Frame
5	0	118	126	134
5	1	121	129	137
5	2	124	132	140
5	3	127	135	143
5	4	131	139	147
5	5	134	142	150
5	6	138	146	154
5	7	142	150	158
5	8	145	154	162
5	9	150	158	166
5	10	154	162	170
5	11	158	166	176
6	0	164	172	182
6	1	170	178	188
6	2	178	184	194
6	3	184	190	200

ing at a scale that goes up and, sometimes, down, for no particular reason that you can determine.

The Goal Range simply says that, instead of demanding of yourself that you weigh in at one particular weight each day, you choose a *range* of pounds that is okay with you. ·

So, for instance, if your Goal Weight is 110, as is mine, according to The Diet Workshop Chart for a 4'11" person, dressed, small frame, I consider my weight to be A-ok if I weigh between 110 and 112. In general, women, especially women 5'4" and under, should limit their range to 2 pounds; taller women and men may elect a 3-pound range.

Choose your range *now*. Add it to the number you've inscribed on the title page as your goal.

You will be happily surprised, relieved, and delighted at the comfort you will derive in your life *après* dieting by using a Goal Range of pounds to live within rather than working at the impossible task of being at the exact same weight every day.

Weighing In

How many times have you gone on a diet, weighed yourself at the very beginning (probably groaned at the number you saw!), and then begun the ritual of "hopping on and off the scale" every other minute? Do you remember the discouragement you felt when the scale did not register at the exact number you expected? On the Wild Weekend Diet it is very important not to weigh yourself constantly (by constantly we mean morning, noon, and night, seven days a week).

Give yourself a break—give your body the time it needs to show a true weight loss. People who get up every morning and head straight for the scale are often in for disappointment. Certainly your true weight is in the morning, before you eat or drink anything, and without clothing. So weigh yourself when you begin the diet, today! Then weigh yourself on Saturday mornings once a week, using the *same scale each time,* and if it is the spring-type, be sure the scale is in the same place each time. Saturday is the best day because you will see the results of the Weekday Slimdown Plan (WSP) as weight loss on the scale. You will then enjoy the Wild Weekend you have earned. *Do not weigh yourself on Monday!* You may get the urge—but resist it!

Questions and Answers
About the Weekday Slimdown Plan

Question: I hate to be told what to eat, let alone when to eat it. Do I have to follow the WSP in order? May I mix and match the days?

Answer: You may exchange any one whole day's plan for another. Each day on the WSP is equal in calories to all the others. You may even eat the same foods every day. However, for nutrition insurance, we recommend you eat a wide variety of foods on the WSP.

Question: I'm working the night shift and always eating on a different schedule from my family. Can I eat the dinner meal at lunchtime and the lunch meal at dinner time?

Answer: Yes. You may arrange your daily meals in any order that fits into your particular life-style. Just be sure to limit your eating to those foods recommended for any given day.

Question: Even though I have been dieting for several years, I still have trouble choosing restaurants that fit my diet. Help me, please!

Answer: Not every restaurant will fit your diet. You'll have most trouble in ethnic restaurants and fast-food places without salad bars. Think about going to plain, American-type restaurants while you are on the WSP. Check the Yellow Pages or a restaurant guide for your area. Call them and ask if they have a salad bar, serve turkey breast, broiled fish, or poultry. Then make your decision as to where you will eat. Plan WSP restaurant eating ahead of time—do not wait until you arrive hungry, when you are most likely to eat whatever they serve.

P.S. Don't hesitate about calling the restaurant. They would rather hear from you and get your business than have you worry and stay away. And they're used to getting calls. People whose health depends on what they eat, such as people with diabetes, ulcers, colitis, and other digestive diseases, allergies, and other problems call because the penalty of eating the wrong foods is more long-lasting than the temporary discomfort of making the call.

Question: I don't like grapefruit or oranges. They make my mouth pucker. You require a citrus fruit every day. Is there something I can eat instead?

Answer: Yes, you can substitute eight ounces of tomato juice for these fruits. Tomatoes and tomato juice are high in vitamin C, as are the citrus fruits.

Question: I've read a lot about dieting and the effects of caffeine, but I really like the taste of real coffee. Do I have to give up my "cuppa" on this diet?

Answer: Caffeine is a drug found in all coffee and most teas. For the dieter a cup of coffee has historically been used as a hunger chaser. In reality the caffeine in the coffee and tea stimulates the production of insulin into the bloodstream, which sets off a feeling of hunger. You are better off drinking decaffeinated coffee and tea and diet beverages as much as possible. However, one or two cups of real coffee per day is acceptable.

Question: I am really a very thirsty person. I drink about thirteen cups of liquid a day. May I drink as much sugar-free soda as I like?

Answer: Yes, and particularly now that many diet sodas are sweetened with aspartame (NutraSweet), you need not worry about the bloating caused by the excessive use of sodium saccharin used to sweeten diet sodas. By the way, it's a good idea for everyone to drink 8 glasses of liquid a day and not less than 6.

Question: I am what you might call the original "cookie monster." When I am dieting, I need to snack on raw vegetables in the middle of the afternoon or I look for cookies. Can I do this on the WSP?

Answer: Plan for an alternative to an afternoon snack habit. Try drinking hot beverages or a diet soda or take a walk instead. If all else fails, eat a salad made of lettuce, cucumbers, and tomatoes.

P.S. If you are following the WSP as directed, you probably won't experience much hunger in the middle of the afternoon.

Question: Not a week goes by that I don't have at least one social event or business function to go to. If I start the WSP on Monday and have to eat a high-calorie meal at a banquet or business dinner on Wednesday, will I blow my diet?

Answer: You don't "have to" eat a high-calorie meal on Wednesday, regardless of where you might be. Look closely at the meal and eat only the foods that fit into your diet plan for that day. If there are none, eat the salad (ask for a double without dressing), order plenty of club soda and decaffeinated coffee, and eat your meal when you get home. Remember, the success of the diet depends on following the WSP exactly as written. Hang in there! The Wild Weekend is coming!

Question: Believe it or not, I sometimes don't want to eat as much as my food plan allows. If I eat less one day during the week, can I add the balance of that day's menu to the next day's menu?

Answer: No. If you don't eat all the foods recommended on any given day, forget them and follow the next day's plan exactly as it is written with no additions.

Question: I have a vegetable garden, and growing tomatoes is my specialty. However, I am not crazy about eating raw vegetables. I notice that you permit tomatoes to be eaten as desired in a salad for lunch and dinner. May I eat tomatoes, cooked as desired?

Answer: Yes. You may eat as many tomatoes as you desire, cooked or raw.

Question: I enjoy eggs for breakfast, but if I can't fry them in butter, they seem dry and rubbery. Any suggestions?

Answer: You may use a nonstick spray to fry or scramble your eggs. Or, if you like a moister egg, try poaching it in boiling water, tomato juice, V-8 juice, or bouillon.

Question: Okay, I am giving up my sauces and gravies while I am on the WSP, but do I have to give up flavor altogether?

Answer: Absolutely not. Use a variety of herbs, spices, and seasonings. You will not be giving up flavor—just calories. Try new combinations: dill or rosemary on chicken; garlic powder and a sprinkle of vinegar on turkey; a small dash of grated Parmesan cheese and butter-flavored powder on fish; and use parsley and paprika to "dress up" your entrées.

Question: Lemon is listed in the Extras section of the WSP. How can I use it?

Answer: Use lemons and limes to flavor and enhance your meals. Sprinkle it on fresh vegetables, fish, and chicken. Fresh or reconstituted lemon may be used to make lemonade. Sweeten it with artificial sweetener. Spice up your tea with a fresh lemon wedge and make a refreshing summer cooler with sparkling water and fresh lemon or lime (or both) wedges.

Question: My husband and I have a predinner cocktail hour every day. He doesn't like it when I don't join him. What can I do while on the WSP?

Answer: First of all, you make the drinks. Give him his usual, and give yourself some sparkling water perked up with lemon or lime. Or, use your fruit allowance, and make yourself a Virgin Mary or Blameless Screwdriver. Join him socially, but save the alcohol calories for the weekend.

Question: The supermarkets are flooded now with all brands of low-calorie margarines. Is it allowed on the WSP for breakfast toast?

Answer: No fats, butter, or margarine are permitted on the WSP. Even though the new low-calorie brands do save you calories, they will still add extra, nonnutritional calories to your WSP. Use diet jelly to moisten and sweeten your breakfast toast.

Question: My sister is on the Wild Weekend Diet. She says she doesn't have to eat all the foods on the WSP. She says she will lose faster if she doesn't. Is this true?

Answer: No, she probably will not lose weight faster and, in the process, will harm herself by eating less than is recommended on the WSP. There are not a lot of calories on the WSP, and the foods recommended are packed with nutritional value. If there appears to be too much food for her, advise her to cut back on the amount of salad she is eating and concentrate on the vegetables and chicken, fish, and other protein.

Question: The Wild Weekend Diet is the best diet I have ever seen. You allow two breads per day on the WSP. (Some diets I have been on don't allow any bread, and I am a breadaholic!) What kinds of breads may I have on the WSP?

Answer: Any bread that has no fruit or nuts in it is permitted. You may select from white, whole wheat, rye, pumpernickel, English muffins, pocket bread, in one-ounce servings two times daily. Avoid the raisin, banana, and date-nut breads until the Wild Weekend. We're glad you think the Wild Weekend Diet is the best; we do, too!

Question: My teenage daughter needs to lose weight. I would like her to go on this diet with me, but there don't seem to be enough calories for her on the WSP. What do you suggest for teenagers on the WSP?

Answer: Teenagers can go on the Wild Weekend Diet very safely. Teenage bodies are still growing and developing and, therefore, require more calories daily than the mature adult. For nutritional well-being, additional foods have been pre-selected and added to the WSP and to the WWD. For this reason, teenagers have more to eat than adults do, but fewer Wild Weekend Units.

Monday through Friday, teenagers will follow the WSP. Girls will add daily: 2 eight-ounce glasses of skim milk or buttermilk *and* 2 apples or oranges. Boys will add daily: 3 eight-ounce glasses of skim milk or buttermilk, 2 ounces cooked meat, fish, or poultry, 1 ounce bread, 2 apples or oranges, *and* 8 ounces tomato juice or 1/2 grapefruit.

On Saturday, teenagers will choose the Saturday breakfast, the Saturday lunch, the food additions above, and 14 WWUs. On Sunday, teenagers may have 7 WWUs for Sunday brunch, the food additions above, and the Sunday dinner.

Use the following chart to help your teenager lose weight on the Wild Weekend Diet!

TEENAGE GIRLS	TEENAGE BOYS
MONDAY–FRIDAY	
Follow WSP and add:	Follow WSP and add:
2 8-ounce glasses skim milk or buttermilk	3 8-ounce glasses skim milk or buttermilk
2 apples or oranges	2 ounces cooked meat, fish, or poultry

1 ounce bread
2 apples or oranges
8 ounces tomato juice or 1/2
  grapefruit

SATURDAY

Saturday breakfast:

1 egg or 1/4 cup cottage
  cheese
1 ounce bread
1/2 cup orange or grapefruit
  juice

and

Saturday lunch:

Lettuce
Tomatoes
3 ounces chicken or 3
  ounces turkey breast
1 ounce bread
1/2 cup berries or 1/2 cup
  fruit packed in its own
  juice

and

Saturday night:

14 Wild Weekend Units

and (anytime)

2 8-ounce glasses skim milk
  or buttermilk
2 apples or oranges

Saturday breakfast:

1 egg or 1/4 cup cottage
  cheese
1 ounce bread
1/2 cup orange or grapefruit
  juice

and

Saturday lunch:

Lettuce
Tomatoes
3 ounces chicken or 3
  ounces turkey breast
1 ounce bread
1/2 cup berries or 1/2 cup
  fruit packed in its own
  juice

and

Saturday night:

14 Wild Weekend Units

and (anytime)

3 8-ounce glasses skim milk
  or buttermilk
2 ounces cooked meat, fish,
  or poultry
1 ounce bread
2 apples or oranges
8 ounces tomato juice or 1/2
  grapefruit

SUNDAY

Brunch:

7 Wild Weekend Units

and

Sunday dinner:

6 ounces plain chicken or
fish, broiled or baked
1/2 cup peas or a small
baked potato, salad, and
1/2 cup water-packed fruit

and

2 8-ounce glasses skim milk
or buttermilk
2 apples or oranges

Brunch:

7 Wild Weekend Units

and

Sunday dinner:

6 ounces plain chicken or
fish, broiled or baked
1/2 cup peas or a small
baked potato, salad, and
1/2 cup water-packed fruit

and

3 8-ounce glasses skim milk
or buttermilk
2 ounces cooked meat, fish,
or poultry
1 ounce bread
2 apples or oranges
8 ounces tomato juice or 1/2
grapefruit

Question: As soon as I decide to lose weight, I become a "scale hopper." Sometimes I weigh myself four or five times a day. Often I am disappointed, even though I have been true-blue to my diet. How often should I weigh myself?

Answer: Once a week is recommended. Your body's weight changes daily (and many times during the same day) for many reasons. To accurately measure weight loss, you need to weigh yourself on the same scale, at the same time, on the same day of each week. Avoid that temptation to weigh yourself every day to measure your success. Instead, measure your success by acknowledging all the changes you are making in your daily eating habits.

Question: I have high blood pressure and have to take medication to control it. Because of this medication, my doctor told me to eat a banana and drink eight ounces of orange juice every day. He told me never to omit these. What can I do on the WSP?

Answer: Follow your doctor's advice and eat the banana and drink the eight ounces of orange juice every day. If you consider these as your total fruit intake for the day, they will not interfere with your weight loss.

Question: I live with a very thin husband and three skinny teenagers! When they are munching on cookies and candy and snacks, I feel very left out of my family's activity and I really don't want to learn to do without this family snack time. What do you suggest?

Answer: Save a fruit for that time. Cut it up into small, bite-size pieces and put a toothpick in each piece. Freeze these fruit pieces for extra crunchiness and sweetness. Try freezing a fruit-flavored diet soda into ice cubes and suck on them for another crunchy and sweet snack choice.

CHAPTER 5

Restaurant Wild Weekends

When a man or a woman is unfaithful to his or her diet, the most frequently named corespondent is that villain Eating Out. Sit down at a table not your own, and the temptation, the agonized choices, the exotic preparations, the convivial atmosphere, all play a part in doing the diet in. The Wild Weekend Diet is designed to position you for success. In this chapter we will acquaint you with the hazards of restaurant eating, tell you how to meet and jump over the hurdles, and show you how to make choices that fit into your Wild Weekend Unit allowance.

Dress for Success

Just as you need a special outfit for your evening out, you also need special messages on your "holiday from dieting" to protect your weight loss.

Start talking to yourself early in the day. Talk about breakfast and lunch. Use these messages to overcome your temptation to skip your No-Think breakfast and lunch. Convince yourself that skipping meals and "saving" calories is harmful to the health of your diet. Your body needs energy to keep on going and to burn up your fat.

Gift yourself with positive thinking. Tell yourself that you can do it, that you can stick to your WWU budget, and that you'll enjoy yourself at the same time.

We all have willpower. Some of us will ourselves to stay on our diet while others of us will ourselves off our diet or to lose the diet battle. But you can be a winner. Think about what you're getting in terms of your choice of wonderful foods to eat, and don't dwell on the fact that you have to practice some restraint and control. When you assert yourself to yourself, you have the power to reach all your goals.

There's more that you can do to get ready for the high point of the diet week. Decide in advance what you'll eat. This is easy if you're going to a familiar restaurant. You know the menu, so you can zero in on what you'll order from soup through dessert. For an evening out in an unfamiliar setting you can make some preliminary decisions on how you will spend your WWUs. Will it be drinks? How many? Or instead, do you opt for a sumptuous entrée or a fabulous dessert?

If you take the time and make the effort to think about the meal before the moment of truth, your success is guaranteed!

Being There

The lure of the restaurant assails all your senses. At the door you're greeted by and surrounded with the aromas of all the foods you love. Bountiful trays of beautifully prepared food fill your eyes. From the moment you step into the room you're involved in the eating experience.

Eating possibilities raise their tempting heads the minute you sit down. Special breads, crisp breadsticks, savory crackers—and butter, their trusty sidekick—are within your reach. You already know it's okay to eat what you want on the Wild Weekend Diet, as long as you count WWUs as you munch along. As you place your drink order, keep adding your WWUs. If your addition is poor, you don't flunk; you just get left behind, stuck at a weight place you don't like.

Temptations abound at the dinner table. The bread basket is bottomless. Others offer you a bite of this or that, and then there's dessert. Ah, dessert! All is okay as long as these samples and tastes appear in your total. Let it be your maxim that "I will be led into temptation, and I will give in to temptation as long as I count the food in my WWU total, even if I eat only a forkful, *and* as long as I am within my WWU budget."

The arrival of the menu is another test of your commitment. Here's where you exercise your freedom of choice as you balance the foods you want against the WWUs you have to spend. Now figure the total from appetizer to drink, through to dessert, so that you'll enjoy the whole experience in comfort, knowing that you're staying within the limits you have set for yourself.

Expect that each and every food you eat in a restaurant has added calories hidden in its preparation. As chefs offer flair and flavor, so also do they offer butter and cream and other ingredients that are hard to determine and therefore difficult to count up. You won't go wrong if you add 2 WWUs just for walking in the door. In fact, you'll be doing your diet and your get-slim plan a big favor.

Here is a glossary of common menu terms. Knowing what they mean will be helpful in ordering and in keeping an accurate count. Particular high-calorie ingredients in the "Meaning" column are in italics.

TERM	MEANING
A la king	Chopped food, primarily chicken or turkey, in *cream* sauce
A la mode	Dessert topped with *ice cream*
Al dente	Pasta cooked until tender yet firm
Amandine	Made or served with *almonds* or other *nuts*
Au gratin	Food that's browned in oven or broiler, topped with *buttered bread crumbs* and *cheese*
Au jus	Meat served in its own juice
Beurre	"Butter" in French
Bourguignon	Foods prepared in *Burgundy wine sauce,* which usually includes *butter* and *cream*

TERM	MEANING
Brûlé	"Burned" in French. Term used to describe food glazed with caramelized *sugar*
Café au lait	Coffee with milk or *cream*
Cappucino	Steamed whole milk with espresso added
Cordon bleu	Filled with *ham* and *cheese*
Crepe	A thin pancake
En brochette	Food that is cooked on a skewer
En cocotte	Cooked in a casserole
En croûte	Wrapped in or topped with a *crust*, usually pastry
Flambé	Desserts soaked in *liquor* and set ablaze
Fricassee	Poultry that is cooked in *sauce* after being browned in oil
Fromage	"Cheese" in French
Julienne	Food cut in thin strips
Marinated	Foods soaked in a liquid mixture for several hours until the food absorbs the flavor. Often *oil* is part of the marinade or mixture.
Poisson	"Fish" in French
Poulet	"Chicken" in French
Provençale	Dishes that are cooked and served with onion, garlic, and *olive oil*
Ragoût	A hearty stew, in thick *gravy*
Sautéed	Pan-fried in a small amount of hot *oil* or *butter*

Bigger Is Not Better

It's time to share some typical restaurant menus along with the WWU analysis of each food. But before we do that there is one thing you must be aware of: the portion size served. In Chapter 3, "Off for the Weekend," we told you that WWUs are computed on the basis of three criteria: type of food, portion size, and method of preparation. Don't give yourself permission to ignore the size of what is served to you. If you want to eat a lot, go to it, as long as you can "afford" to do so.

Sample Meal Plans

Each of the following menus is based on 24 or fewer WWUs. That means that each of the menus would suit a woman's Saturday Night Wild Weekend Unit Budget, and if you're a man, you still have 7 additional WWUs to spend. These counts were derived by taking the WWU value for each food item in the menu and keeping a running total on the meal. The sources used are the Food Lists in Chapters 7, 8, and 9.

The meals include a world of food choices, and they show you the many different ways you can choose WWUs that suit your taste. You'll find sample menus from Italian restaurants to French bistros, from Greek tavernas to Indian kitchens, as well as from Chinese, Japanese, American, fast-food restaurants, and many others. You may follow these menu plans exactly, or you can use them as learning models as to what costs what in Wild Weekend Units.

The WWU value for all entrées was figured in a three-step process:

1. First we took the WWU value for six ounces of cooked meat, fish, poultry, eggs, or cheese.
2. To this total we added the WWU value for the method of preparation (Hot List items).
3. Finally we added WWUs for any additions to the entrée, such as sauces, gravies, creams, stuffing, or cheese or bread toppings (again, Hot List items).

The WWU value for all other courses was calculated by totaling calories found in standard recipes and converting the calories to WWUs based on an average serving.

MENUS
Foreign Restaurants

FRENCH RESTAURANT #1	WWUS
Pouilly-Fuissé, 1 glass	2
Soupe à l'Oignon	3
Salade Niçoise	4
Escargots à la Bourguignon (snails with garlic butter, 3)	2
Sole Bretonne	4
French bread, plain, 1 piece	1
Chocolate mousse	7
Coffee, black	0
	23

FRENCH RESTAURANT #2	WWUS
Champagne cocktail, 1	3
Artichoke Heart salad	2
Beef Bourguignon	8
Peas	1
French garlic bread, 1 slice	3
Champagne sorbet	5
Benedictine and brandy	2
Coffee, black	0
	24

ITALIAN RESTAURANT #1	WWUS
Chianti wine, 2 glasses	4
Minestrone soup, 1 cup	3
Tossed salad with vinegar and lemon	0
Italian bread, 1 slice, plain	2

Spaghetti or Linguine Carbonara	12
Broccoli, cooked in garlic and oil	3
Coffee, black	0
	24

ITALIAN RESTAURANT #2	WWUS
Manhattan, 1	2
Chablis wine, 2 glasses	4
Clams Casino, 2	4
Lasagna	8
Italian bread, 1 slice, with 1 tablespoon butter	3
Zabaglione	2
Espresso	0
	23

GREEK RESTAURANT #1	WWUS
Stuffed grape leaf	2
Trahana noodle soup	3
Roast leg of lamb with Orzo	8
Pilaf Kapama	3
Peas	1
Baklava	5
Coffee, black	0
	22

GREEK RESTAURANT #2	WWUS
Beer, light, 12 ounces	1
Greek salad	7
Souvlaki	10
Carrots	0

	WWUS
Bread, 1 piece, with 1 table-spoon butter	3
Semolina cake, 2" square	3
Coffee, black	0
	24

INDIAN RESTAURANT #1

	WWUS
Chablis wine, 2 glasses	4
Crab Malabar	2
Houmus, 2 tablespoons	2
Syrian bread, 1 small pocket	1
Raita (cucumber and yogurt salad)	2
Tandoori Chicken	4
Palak Paneer, 1/2 cup	2
Turmeric potatoes	2
Cream pudding	4
Coffee with cream and sugar, 1 cup	1
	24

INDIAN RESTAURANT #2

	WWUS
Martini, 1	2
Mulligatawny soup	2
Tabouli, 4 tablespoons	3
Syrian bread, 1 small pocket	1
Fried filet of sole	8
Obla Saag (cooked spinach)	0
Indian fried rice	2
Ande Ki Kari	3

Bread pudding	3
Coffee, black	0
	24

JAPANESE RESTAURANT #1	WWUS
Mai Tai cocktail, 2	6
Nuta-ae (seafood and scallion salad in Miso dressing)	2
Hamaguri Ushiojitate (clear clam soup with mushrooms)	0
Sashimi, 10 pieces	5
Chicken Teriyaki	5
Gohan (steamed white rice), 1 cup	3
Ginger ice cream	2
Tea	0
	23

JAPANESE RESTAURANT #2	WWUS
Black Belt (Kahlua and sake), 1	3
Samo Yoshino-Ni (duck in sake-seasoned sauce)	10
Miso-Ni (mackerel in Miso sauce)	4
Gohan (steamed white rice), 1 cup	3
Fresh pineapple chunks, 1 cup	2
Tea	0
	22

CHINESE RESTAURANT #1	WWUS
Planter's Punch cocktail	3
Egg roll, 1	2

	WWUS
Barbecued spareribs, 2	4
Pork strips, 3	2
Beef Chop Suey, 1/2 cup	2
Lobster Cantonese, 1/2 cup	4
Pork fried rice, 1/2 cup	3
Almond cookies, 2	3
Pineapple chunks, 1/2 cup	1
Tea	0
	24

CHINESE RESTAURANT #2	WWUS
Daiquiri, 1	2
Wonton or Hot and Sour Soup	3
Egg Foo Yong, 1 patty with gravy	3
Stir-fried chicken, 1 cup	7
Moo Goo Gai Pan, 2 cups	7
Fortune cookies, 2	1
Tea	0
	23

AMERICAN RESTAURANT #1	WWUS
Old Fashioned cocktail, 1	2
Madeira wine spritzer, 1	2
New England clam chowder, 1/2 cup	2
Salad with lemon	0
Sole Véronique	12
Cauliflower, steamed	0
Potato, boiled, with 1 table-spoon each butter and sour cream	3

Chocolate pudding, 1/2 cup	3
Coffee, black	0
	24

American Restaurant #2   wwus

Rob Roy, 2	4
Consommé	0
Tossed salad with 2 tablespoons French dressing	2
Veal chops, broiled	8
Baked squash	1
Bread, 2 slices, with 2 table-spoons butter	5
Triple Sec	2
Tea with lemon and sugar, 2 cups	1
	23

Fast-Food Restaurants

Burger King   wwus

Salad bar, 1 platter, full choice of all items, with 2 table-spoons bleu cheese dressing	5
Cheeseburger	4
French fries, small order	3
Chocolate shake	4
Apple pie	4
	20

BURGER KING	WWUS
Salad bar, vegetables only, with 1 tablespoon croutons and 1 tablespoon low-calorie dressing	2
Whopper Junior	4
French fries, small order	3
Onion rings	4
Diet soda	0
	13

WENDY'S	WWUS
Salad bar, 1 platter, full choice of all items, with 2 tablespoons Italian dressing	5
Triple Cheeseburger	12
French fries, regular order	4
Diet soda	0
	21

McDONALD'S	WWUS
Big Mac	7
French fries, large	5
Caramel sundae	4
McDonaldland cookies	4
Root beer, 16-ounce size	3
	23

KENTUCKY FRIED CHICKEN	WWUS
3-piece crispy dinner	14
Corn	2
Roll	2

Butter, 1 tablespoon	2
Coffee with cream and sugar, 1 cup	1
	21

Fish House   wwus

Dark draft beer, 12 ounces	2
Clam Chowder, New England-style	3
Crab cocktail with sauce	2
Codfish cakes, 2	3
Fried scallops, 10 average-size	3
Cole slaw, 1/2 cup	2
Potato salad	3
French fries, 10 pieces	2
	20

Kosher Deli   wwus

Bagels, 2	8
Cream cheese, 1/4 cup	5
Lox, 4 ounces	4
Potato salad, 1/2 cup	3
Cole slaw, 1/2 cup	3
Coffee, black	0
	23

Coffee Shop   wwus

Grilled Reuben	7
Greek salad	7
Potato chips, 1 ounce	2

	WWUS
Chocolate éclair	3
Chocolate milk shake	5
	24

MEXICAN	WWUS
Margarita, strawberry, 1	3
Guacamole dip, 1/2 cup	3
Tortilla chips, 2 ounces	4
Burrito	5
Refried beans, 1/2 cup	3
Flan (caramel custard)	4
Coffee	0
	22

PIZZA PLACE	WWUS
Beer, regular, 3 12-ounce bottles	6
Tossed salad with 3 tablespoons Italian dressing	6
Pizza, cheese, 10″ pie, 1	12
Diet soda	0
	24

BUFFET #1—COLD	WWUS
Champagne, 1 glass	2
Tossed salad (predressed)	3
Roll, small, with butter	3
Roast beef, 1-ounce slice	2
Swiss cheese, 1-ounce wedge	2
Salmon salad, 1/4 cup	1
Tuna salad, 1/4 cup	2
Cole slaw, 1/2 cup	2

Potato salad, 1/2 cup	3
Ladyfingers, 3	2
Fruit gelatin	2
Coffee	0
	24

BUFFET #2—HOT	WWUS
Burgundy wine, 1 glass	2
Beef Stroganoff with buttered noodles, 1/2 cup	8
Spareribs, 3	3
Chicken wings, 2	3
Sweet-and-Sour Meatballs, 3	3
Peach cobbler	2
Tea	0
	21

Brunches

Sunday brunch is your second opportunity to embark on a food adventure. If you're a woman, you have 12 WWUs to spend on brunch; if you're a man, you have 14.

If you're asking yourself whether you will lose weight if you spend these extra WWUs on a Sunday brunch, the answer is yes, you will. Remember, you saved WWUs all week long to be spent on the Wild Weekend!

HOTEL AND RESTAURANT BRUNCH #1	WWUS
Bloody Mary	2
Bagel	3
Cream cheese, 2 tablespoons	4

	WWUS
Smoked fish, 2 ounces	2
Coffee	0
	11

HOTEL AND RESTAURANT BRUNCH #2

	WWUS
Mimosa	3
French toast, 1 slice	2
Bacon, 2 strips	2
Poached egg, 1	1
Maple syrup, 2 tablespoons	2
Coffee	0
	10

HOTEL AND RESTAURANT BRUNCH #3

	WWUS
Screwdriver	3
Fresh fruit cup	1
Eggs Benedict	7
Tea	0
	11

HOTEL AND RESTAURANT BRUNCH #4

	WWUS
Cape Codder	2
Eggs, fried, 2	5
Sausage, 1 link	1
Coffee	0
	8

Fast-Food Brunches

McDonald's

	WWUS
Egg McMuffin	4
Hash browns, 1 patty	3
Orange juice, 6 ounces	2
Coffee w/cream and sugar, 2 cups	2
	11

McDonald's

	WWUS
Hotcakes with butter and syrup	7
Grapefruit juice	2
Milk, 8 ounces	2
	11

Deli

	WWUS
Corned Beef sandwich, 4 ounces meat on hard roll	10
Dill pickles	0
Diet soda	0
	10

Coffee Shop

	WWUS
Open roast beef sandwich with gravy	5
Mashed potatoes, 1/2 cup	2
Lettuce and tomato	0
Soft-serve vanilla ice milk, 1 cup	2
Milk, whole, 8 ounces	2
	11

Here are some tips for eating out from Laura W., who was one of the test dieters who lost weight very well on the Wild Weekend Diet:

"Relax! This diet is going to work for you. Be informed! After you and your friend, lover, or spouse have decided to go out for dinner or brunch, choose the restaurant. Take some time during the week and call ahead to find out how they prepare their entrées. If you know in advance that you are going to eat veal parmigiana because it is your favorite Italian food, you can plan your Wild Weekend meal in advance. If you are going to a familiar restaurant and you are not crazy about the way they prepare their entrées, you can have your fish or chicken broiled plain and then splurge on a favorite dessert like Baked Alaska. Use the Weekday Slimdown Plan as your bible during the week, then you can be comfortable and feel entitled to spend your Wild Weekend Units on Saturday night.

"Be flexible! You can change your mind. When you look over the menu, you may have a change of heart and decide you want a totally different meal from the one you planned. This is okay. Just remember the basic rules of adding Wild Weekend Units for cooking methods (Hot List) and that WWU values are for six ounces of cooked meat or poultry. Stay within your WWU budget!

"Remember that you are in control. When you are served a meal, you do not have to eat every bite. Eat only until you are comfortably satisfied. After you have eaten approximately half your meal, stop! Put your fork down and pay attention to how your body feels. Ask yourself if you are still hungry. If the answer is yes, eat half of what is left, then stop again and ask yourself once more if you are hungry. When you no longer want more food, push your plate away from you and ask the waiter to remove it. If you cannot summon the attention of the waiter, do what I do. Sprinkle the remains with lots of pepper and salt or sugar. Who wants to pick at prime rib with sugar on it? Yecch!

"You do not have to sample all the food that is on the table or on someone else's plate. If bread is a problem and it's not part of your Wild Weekend Unit budget, move the basket from your reach, or better yet, ask that it be removed from the table.

"Ask that your salad be served with the dressing on the side. When a salad is served with the dressing already on it, usually it adds up to 4 WWUs. If you have your salad served with the dressing on the side, you can reduce the Wild Weekend Units by using less dressing. Each tablespoon of regular dressing adds 2 WWUs. This same principle applies to the butter and/or sour cream on baked potatoes or vegetables. Request that the butter or sour cream be served on the side so that *you* make the decision of how much of these accompaniments you eat.

"Now it's time for dessert. Do you really want it, or are you ordering simply because you've got WWUs left over? Sense how your body is feeling. If you aren't really hungry for dessert, skip it and lose weight a little faster.

"If someone tries to coerce you off your diet and tempt you to eat more than you want, a simple statement I use with great effect is, 'I'm full!'

"Many restaurants, in an attempt at grace, offer nuts, candies, and other little temptations in dishes with spoons. Before you dive into these little devils, stop and think for a minute. It is not possible to have *all* your favorites every weekend and lose weight. I learned this lesson very early in my weight-loss process. Make your choices count. Candies and nuts are outrageously high in calories. The calories and Wild Weekend Units mount up very quickly when you pick at a bowl of mints or at a box of chocolates. Take my advice: Don't stand near the candies or nuts. Engage in conversation with friends who are safely removed from the temptations. Stay close to *thin* friends. The thin friends I mean are those who watch their weight and are successful at it. Imitate them. Look at the little bowls of candy and nuts as bowls of fat (that's what chocolate and nuts contain, although they are attractively and deliciously packaged, aren't they?). Then imagine lumps of fat sticking out on your hips and thighs.

"Be strong! Control your appetite. Remember your desire to be thin! You can have your favorite entrée *and* your favorite dessert. You can have breads and cocktails. You can have many of the foods you enjoy but you can't have everything. Is this big news? In the perfect world that never was on earth you can have everything. In this world, the one we live in, you must make choices. Make your choices *count,* and lose weight!"

Questions and Answers

Question: What is the best advice you can give me before I go out to eat?

Answer: Psych yourself into believing that you will make choices that are good for you. As soon as you have plans to go to a restaurant tell yourself that you will be able to stick to your Wild Weekend Diet. Keep telling yourself this over and over and over. You can do it! Many others have done it before you. Tell yourself that you have wonderful Wild Weekend Units to spend on the foods of your choice and then begin to decide what it is you wish to eat and drink. There are no restrictions on the choices, but there are guidelines to follow. Reread Chapter 4, "Weekday Slimdown Plan," thoroughly to reacquaint yourself with the overall instructions and tips for Wild Weekends. Memorize them. Then:

1. Choose a restaurant that offers a wide variety of foods. Don't limit yourself to a place that serves only fried foods. You may eat something fried, but then, again, you may want something broiled or baked.

2. Call the restaurant ahead of time and ask how the food is prepared. Check to see whether all the vegetables are served in butter and if the entrées are served with sauces and gravies. This is especially important for Greek, Italian, and French restaurants. Knowing beforehand, you can then plan how many WWUs you will be spending *if* and *when* you order these foods. Ask them if they have a salad bar and if they serve diet salad dressing. If they do not, then you can plan to spend WWUs on salad dressing or make the choice to bring diet dressing from home or to eat your salad plain.

3. Use the sample restaurant meal plans earlier in this chapter to map out your menu ahead of time. Then when you're there, you

will know exactly what you will order and how many WWUs you will be spending, and you will spare yourself the discomfort of making on-the-spot decisions. In other words, you order at home just as if you were shopping from a mail-order catalog.

Question: Will I still lose weight if I eat breakfast and lunch on Saturday?

Answer: Yes, you will still lose weight. It is very important that you eat three meals each day on the Wild Weekend Diet, except for Sunday, when we suggest brunch so that your body will have all the energy it needs to burn off its fat.

Question: I encounter a big problem when we're waiting in the cocktail lounge to be seated at the restaurant. When I join my husband for a few drinks before dinner, there is always some type of snack right in front of me. I find these peanuts or pretzels or crackers irresistible. What can I do?

Answer: First of all, make a reservation and arrive just before you are to be seated. Ask your husband if you can have cocktails at the dinner table instead of in the lounge. At your table you have three choices. You may order a cocktail and no snack. Or you may have a club soda or diet soda free of charge (no WWUs). Or you can order a salad and enjoy that while your husband is enjoying his cocktails and appetizers. Of course you may wind up waiting anyway, restaurants not being 100 percent perfect in honoring reservations. If that happens, know that you gave it your best try. *And,* all options are still open to you. If you elect to snack, that's fine, just count your Wild Weekend Units and your diet plan will stay intact. An important thing to remember is that you are not helpless because of the way things have always been in the past. You can change and adopt new thin behaviors. It's up to you!

Question: Whenever I am dieting I find that wine or alcohol hits me very quickly and then I lose control and I begin to pick at everything in sight. Do you have any suggestions?

Answer: This is very common. When you diet, you eat less, and therefore you feel the effects of alcohol more quickly.

To avoid the sudden "high," try watering down your cocktail. Ask

that the liquor be served on the side so that you can pour in as much as
you want at a time. We know of one lady who loves Scotch and soda.
She orders one drink with two glasses of soda. That way the jigger of
Scotch is split between two drinks. You might like a wine spritzer—it's
diluted with soda water. You take longer to finish this tall drink, and
your body has time to absorb the alcohol. A very good tip is to eat
before you drink; even a salad will help your body to absorb the alcohol
more effectively.

Instead of picking at everything in sight, order a shrimp cocktail or a
salad or a fruit cup to eat, or enjoy some cheese and crackers. Before
you go out, decide what you'll eat with your drink, and stick to your
plan.

Question: I have a hard time controlling myself when the bread
basket is placed in front of me on the table. Help!

Answer: Again, on the Wild Weekend Diet you don't have to deny
yourself the foods you love best. Eat some bread! Just count this bread
into your WWUs. You can have your bread and lose weight, too.

Question: There seems to be a tremendous amount of food on the
Wild Weekend Saturday night dinners. Do I have to eat it all? Do I
have to use all my WWUs?

Answer: No, you do not have to spend your total Wild Weekend
allotment. That is your limit, not a "have-to." In fact, as long as you eat
a well-balanced meal that consists of meat, fish, or poultry and a salad
and vegetable, you do not have to eat any more. In fact, you will be
doing your diet a favor by eating fewer WWUs and causing a faster
weight loss.

You need never overeat on the Wild Weekend Diet. The plan was
created for those people who want to eat more on the weekend and for
whom dieting was an ever-long struggle with temptations, which, in the
past, led to failure.

Question: My husband's boss takes us out to dinner very frequently
and he insists that we order big, lavish meals. When I am dieting, I am
put in a very awkward position as I don't want to offend my husband's
boss. Do you have any suggestions?

Answer: Just as big gifts can come in small packages, so, too, can lavish meals come in small calorie counts. To our mind an evening that includes champagne, shrimp cocktail, Caesar salad, lobster, asparagus, and fresh fruit is elegant indeed. The check for this meal is impressive, but the calorie count and, therefore, the WWU value is low.

Question: What do you think of a person who is dieting and orders all kinds of foods from the menu, then only eats half of everything?

Answer: I think that this person is diet-intelligent. This sounds like a person who is serious about losing weight but is intent on not feeling deprived of variety and is willing to put limits on food. Seems like a fun person to have dinner with.

Question: How can I handle a pushy waiter or waitress? It seems as if they are trained to get me to order certain foods when I really don't want them.

Answer: You are very perceptive when you say you think they are trained to behave in such a manner. They are! There are some who are trained how to ask questions in such a way as to receive an order. An example of this is "What can I bring you from the bar?" rather than "Would you care for something from the bar?" or "We have apple, blueberry, or cherry pie, which one do you want?" rather than "Would you like some pie?" They are trained to get you to order. As long as you are aware of their techniques, you can be prepared to answer in a way that suits you and your diet. You can say "Thank you, I'll have the apple pie" and you can also say "Thank you, I don't care for any dessert." Listen to the question, think about whether or not you want dessert, then give the answer *you* want to give.

Question: I think the most difficult part of eating out is ordering from the menu. Everything is so tempting, and there are always foods I cannot prepare at home. How can I avoid going crazy and ordering everything?

Answer: Menus are designed to trigger your appetite. If this is a problem for you, as it is for many of us, you don't have to open the menu. If you have taken the time as suggested to plan your meal at home and count your WWUs so that you remain within your total unit count, you can order from your own list. Be prepared with your own made-at-home menu, and you will succeed.

Question: I guess you could call me a martyr. I never eat anything fattening in front of people when I eat out. But the minute I get home, I go on a crazy binge. I want to stop this, but I don't know how.

Answer: Closet eaters are very common; you are not alone in this action. Many overweight people feel very self-conscious about ordering high-calorie foods in front of others for fear of hearing a remark such as "No wonder she's the size she is, look at what she eats." This is cruel, and it certainly doesn't make you feel terrific.

When you eat lightly in the company of others, you feel deprived because everyone else is eating as they choose. Alone and left out, you may very well go home and comfort yourself with private eating, where no one can see or criticize you. So you see, one of the greatest advantages of the Wild Weekend Diet is that you can eat whatever you want without fear of gaining weight. You won't feel deprived and you won't *be* deprived, nor will you need to go home and binge. You "binge" legally, with family or friends. No more Lone Ranger at the Dining Board.

Question: I am a veteran dieter. I don't ever want to go back to eating butter, sugar, ice cream, and mayonnaise again. These foods are part of the reason I gained weight in the first place. Why do you allow them on your diet?

Answer: There is no such thing as a good or bad food for dieting. All foods have been made available on the Wild Weekend Diet. You have the choice of selecting only the foods you want. Other people may want to enjoy butter, sugar, or mayonnaise because they are foods they miss most on a diet, but you don't have to eat them. You sound like a very strong and determined dieter. Stick to your guns.

CHAPTER 6

Vacations, Birthdays, Holidays, and Other Special Occasions

Vacations

Vacations offer some of us a chance to relax, to take time off from schedules and hassles, a time to let it all hang out, a period to "go with the flow."

For others, vacations are viewed as opportunities for adventure, a period in which to experience the past glories of the Old World or to explore the present excitement of modern world cities.

Whichever mode of vacation suits us best, we all share the experience of vacationing as a departure from our usual routine. A change. A break. A time away.

All of us who diet must decide how to keep our commitment to weight loss and how to deal with our diet regimen during these special and precious days.

Clearly, each of us has a choice. And we need to recognize that we do. We can pack our diet and take it with us on vacation, or we can leave it behind with the rest of our routines and schedules.

Then, too, there's a third choice to explore. We can maintain our weight on vacation. This third choice calls for us to practice some control when we're away so that when we come home, we are rewarded by the numbers on the scale.

Of course, you can ignore all of the above, but that's the worst choice. After all, it is your body and life, and you are responsible for what happens to you whether you are at home or whether you are on vacation. It's your body, your life, and your goals. You owe it to yourself to make up your mind about what you want *most.*

Here in the real world, vacation eating is one eating-out experience after another. Therefore, all the tips we gave you in the previous chapter on restaurant eating apply to vacation eating as well. Additionally, here are some special vacation tips and experiments for you.

- Wherever you go, whatever you do, keep in your mind, at all times, your arrival home, your weighing in. Congratulate yourself on your ability to decide what you want to do.
- Be conscious of your slimming body whether you are sunning on the shore or walking the cities.
- Take along this book. One very clever and successful dieter said, "If I can't leave my fat at home, then I can't leave my diet at home, either!"
- Continue to eat a balanced diet and three meals a day. Good nutrition will help you feel your best while you're on vacation.
- Plan your dining in advance. Broiled fish or chicken will always be a better choice for you than fried foods, vacation or no, diet or not.
- When you're especially hungry, indulge yourself with the vegetables that abound in the city/country/town you're in.
- Ask yourself if you really need cream sauces on vegetables, if you must blow all those calories on Newburgs and French sauces.
- Tote along a "Diet Survival Kit" containing packets of diet dressings and sweeteners. Artificial sweetener is especially handy in foreign countries where diet drinks are often not available.
- When you leave your hotel, pack an orange or an apple in your tote bag, to eat as a snack while sunning on the beach or trotting around the city.
- Order your salad dry, and use your packet of salad dressing or a wedge of lemon to sprinkle over your salad.
- When eating buffet-style, concentrate on shrimp and turkey rather than ham and Swedish meatballs. Better yet, avoid buffets.
- Rehearse your nonchalant way of saying "No, thank you."

- Before you eat anything, ask yourself, "Do I really want this?"
- Plan your itinerary to leave time to relax over meals. Vacation is a good time to get in touch with what's happening in the mind and in the heart of your spouse or traveling companion.
- Develop the fine art of conversation, especially at dessert time. Notice how thin people pass up dessert, and let them be an inspiration to you.
- Eat slowly.
- Chew thoroughly. Savor the flavor of those holiday meals you're paying hard-earned money for.
- If you feel like it, ask for a Virgin Mary, a Bloody Mary without vodka, at brunches or dinners.
- At get-togethers, station yourself next to a thin person. Watching the way thin people eat and drink is inspirational and practical.
- Keep thinking thin.
- Plan your itinerary to include plenty of exercise. Don't just loll around the ship or motel pool; really swim in it every day you're there. Take time out from your busy schedule to play some tennis; don't let your game get rusty.
- Make sure your sight-seeing includes plenty of good, healthy walking. Walk briskly to increase the calorie burn-up.
- Reward yourself for good, diet-conscious behavior by buying yourself something wonderful and non-caloric.
- Be careful not to get overtired. Fatigue weakens your willpower.
- You don't have to eat all that you paid for. Give yourself permission to get what you really want from your vacation. Above all, have a good time!

Birthdays, Holidays, and Other Special Occasions

Every day is somebody's something.

Just think about it. If it's not your birthday or anniversary, then it's probably someone else's special occasion, or will be shortly. If you're searching for an excuse to go off your diet, it's not difficult to find one.

We dedicate the following information (ammunition you will need to combat the external excuses) so that you can accomplish your goal. You *can* succeed in the face of eating agendas—yours and those of everybody else in the munching world.

At-Home Occasions

"I made your favorite dessert."

"Try just one."

"One won't hurt."

"You look fine to me."

Our social whirl is so often an eating world, isn't it? And sometimes other people have a hard time enjoying themselves when they know you're holding back. Whatever the psychological reasons for this, the phenomenon is true. And so they try to persuade you from your goals. What you need to remember here is how you'll feel best. And that means the day after as well as at the moment. Here are some things to remember when you are visiting:

1. You *never* have to eat to please someone else.
2. The Wild Weekend Diet permits you to spend your WWUs in any way you'd like.
3. Be aware of portion sizes and specific Wild Weekend Unit counts of all foods you eat.
4. Eating before you go to someone's home is a standard diet lifesaver.
5. While at the party pile on the salad, drink plenty of sparkling water, and talk, talk, talk throughout the entire meal.
6. Keep track of your WWUs as you eat them.
7. On some level be aware of your strategies and goals at all times.

The following are some sample foods that might be offered at home parties. Their Wild Weekend Units have been calculated from the base information in Chapters 7, 8, and 9. In other words, the following food values are listed either in those chapters or the recipes have been broken down to yield the Wild Weekend Unit count.

At-Home Special Occasion Wild Weekends

SATURDAY NIGHT COMPANY/ BIRTHDAYS/ANNIVERSARIES	WWUS
White wine spritzer, 2	4
Pretzelettes, 20 pieces	1
Cheddar cheese, 1½ ounce	2
Meatballs, homemade, 3 ounces	3
Lasagna	8
Salad with fresh lemon	0
Zucchini	0
Chocolate cake, frosted	5
Coffee	0
	23

GRADUATIONS/SHOWERS	WWUS
Bloody Mary, 2	4
Potato chips, 15	2
Deli platter:	
Turkey breast, 2 ounces	2
Roast beef, 2 ounces	4
American Cheese, 1 ounce	1
Roll and mustard	2
Pickles, sweet mixed, 1 ounce	1
Salad with 2 tablespoons Italian dressing	3
White cake, with frosting	4
	23

BACKYARD BARBECUES	WWUS
Beer, light, 24 ounces (2 cans)	2
Hot dog with bun	4
Hamburger with bun	7
Potato salad, 1/2 cup	3
Cole slaw, 1/2 cup	3
Salad, plain	0
Marshmallows, 4 large	2
Watermelon, 6" × 11/2"	2
Diet soda	0
	23

SUNDAY FAMILY DINNER/ EASTER/ CHRISTMAS/THANKSGIVING	WWUS
Brandy eggnog	5
Roast turkey, 6 ounces	4
Stuffing, 1/4 cup	2
Gravy, homemade, 1/4 cup	2
Mashed potatoes, 1/2 cup	2
Boiled onions, 1/2 cup	1
Cranberry sauce, 2 tablespoons	1
Roll, plain	2
Pumpkin pie	3
Whipped cream, 2 tablespoons	1
Coffee	0
	23

PASSOVER SEDER	WWUS
Wine, sweet, 1 glass	4
Chopped liver, 2 tablespoons	2
Gefilte fish, 2 ounces	4
Matzo, 1 board	2

Chicken soup	1
Salad with 2 tablespoons low-calorie French dressing	1
Turkey breast, 6 ounces	4
String beans	0
Jell-O mold dessert, 1/2 cup	2
Honey Cake, 1/12th home recipe	2
Coffee with sugar and nondairy creamer, 2 cups	2
	24

The Catered Affair

Weddings, special anniversary parties, and graduations are some of the happy occasions that take place outside a home environment. As the number of guests can vary from ten to the hundreds, so, too, can the courses run from four to ten.

Generally, though, the catered affair is easier on the dieter. For starters, host and hostess will be socializing, not pressing food on each and every guest, not chasing you down the hall with the Baked Alaska, so the pressure is off. Also, there is, generally, little opportunity for second helpings.

It's likely, though, that you'll still need to assert yourself from time to time. You know how to do that by now. And, best of all, you have your WWUs to spend, so it should be a wonderful affair. To help you along, here are some hints:

- Don't eat what you don't want to eat.
- Ask for meat and salads without gravies and dressings, if that's the way you'd like to eat them. The WWU choices are still up to you to make.
- Eat only what you planned to eat.
- Stop eating when you feel satisfied.

- When you're finished, make a trip to the bathroom and brush your teeth and freshen up. With a little luck, your plate will be gone by the time you return.
- Don't eat food you don't like. Make this a diet maxim of yours. *Make this a lifetime maxim of yours.*
- Call the caterer. This is easier than speaking directly with the hostess. Tell him or her that you will be a guest at the _____ function and you would like to know what will be served. Take out your copy of *Wild Weekend Diet,* get a pencil and a piece of paper, and start allotting your WWUs. Knowing exactly what you will eat and the number of WWUs you will spend, you will be going prepared.
- Check over the following menus so that you'll have an idea of what you might be served and what the foods are worth in WWU counts.

Catered Affair #1	wwus
Whiskey sour, 1	2
Sparkling Burgundy wine, 1 glass	2
Chicken liver puffs, 2 pieces	2
Sirloin steak, broiled, 6 ounces	9
Assorted relish tray	0
Tossed green salad with 2 tablespoons oil and vinegar	3
Mashed potatoes, 1/2 cup	2
Eclair, custard-filled, chocolate icing	3
Coffee	0
	23

CATERED AFFAIR #2	WWUS
Champagne, 1 glass	2
Salad with 2 tablespoons Roquefort dressing	3
Roll with 1 tablespoon butter	3
Prime rib, 6 ounces	10
Potato, baked, with 2 tablespoons sour cream	2
Green beans	0
White cake, iced	4
Coffee	0
	24

CATERED AFFAIR #3	WWUS
Margarita, 1	2
Chicken and rice soup, 1 cup	1
Salad with 1 tablespoon French dressing	1
Roast chicken, 6 ounces	4
Gravy, 1/4 cup	2
Stuffing, 1/4 cup	2
Mashed potatoes, 1/2 cup	2
Apple pie	4
Tea with lemon	0
Brandy, 1 1/2 ounces	2
	20

CATERED AFFAIR #4	WWUS
Champagne, 1 glass	2
Caviar, 2 tablespoons	2
Whole wheat crackers, 4	1
Lobster tail, bread-stuffed	8
Asparagus tips	0

	WWUS
Pecan roll, plain	4
Raspberry shortcake	4
Coffee with Benedictine and Brandy	2
	23

CHAPTER 7

Great Beginnings: Appetizers and Accompaniments

And now to the nitty-gritty of WWU values. This chapter, along with Chapters 8 and 9, lists nearly every food you'll come across on your Wild Weekend, from appetizer to dessert. You'll want to spend time learning how unit values are determined. It's time well spent because when you're through, you'll be able to do an accurate count on anything and everything edible—from the simplest cocktails to elaborate gourmet entrées to heavenly, creamy, gooey, desserts.

Many selections combine two or more ingredients. With simple combinations, we merely took the calorie count available in numerous calorie-counting books and assigned a unit value per serving based on calories. This method applies to breads, muffins, rolls, soups, snacks, salad dressings, vegetables, fruits, and beverages.

For more complicated items we checked basic cookbook recipes, listed all significant ingredients, omitting spices, lemon juice, bouillon, and other substances that are practically without calories and assigned calorie counts to each ingredient. Then we added up the total calories for that recipe. Next we divided the recipe into an average serving size. For the entrées, we figured calories on a 6-ounce cooked portion of meat, fish, or poultry. Finally we assigned a unit value for that serving.

Simple? Most good ideas are. That doesn't mean you have license to assume that the unit values are 100 percent accurate. Recipes from different sources differ in ingredients and in amounts of ingredients.

You can assume that the unit values listed are a good approximation, and remember the Wild Weekend maxim: *You never go wrong when you count high.*

The whole world of food choice is open to you now. Knowledge is power. The following information gives you freedom of choice over what you eat and, ultimately, how you look and feel.

You have the power to do what you want to do, be what you want to be.

APPETIZERS

	WWUS		WWUS
Barbecued spareribs, 3	6	Clams, steamed, 1½ pints, with ¼ cup drawn butter	6
Beef puffs, 2 pieces	2		
Caponata, 1 ounce	3		
Caviar, 1 tablespoon	1	Clams Casino, 1	2
Cheese blintze, home recipe	6	Crab or shrimp cocktail	2
Cheese puffs, 2 pieces	2	Egg roll, 1	2
Cheese straws, 2 pieces	1	Franks, cocktail, in sauce, 1	1
Chicken liver puffs, 2 pieces	2	Franks-in-blankets, 2 pieces	2
Chicken puffs, 2 pieces	2	Gefilte fish, home recipe	4
Chicken wings, fried, 3 pieces	5	Herring, chopped, home recipe	3
Chili con Queso, ¼ cup	3	Herring, kippered, 3½ ounces	3
Chopped liver, chicken, 2 tablespoons	2	Herring, pickled, 3½ ounces	3
Clam cake, 2½-ounce cake	2	Herring, smoked, bloaters, 3½ ounces	3
Clams, steamed, 1½ pints	1	Meat kreplach, 1 home recipe	2

	WWUS		WWUS
Mortadella, 1 ounce	2	Prosciutto, 1 ounce	1
Nachos with cheese and chile peppers, 5	2	Seviche, 1 serving	2
		Shrimp puffs, 2 pieces	2
Oysters, fried, 1 serving	3	Shrimp toast, 1 slice	3
		Tortellini in cream sauce, 1 portion	7
Oysters, raw, 5–8 medium	1	Tostaditas, 13 chips	2
Oysters, scalloped, 6	4	Zucchini or cauliflower, fried, 3 ounces	3
Pork dumplings, 3	4		
Potato skins, fried with cheese, bacon, or sour cream, 1	4		

DIPS

(1 ounce unless noted)

	WWUS		WWUS
Bacon and horseradish	1	Houmus, 2 tablespoons	2
Bacon and smoke	1	Onion	1
Bean, Frito-Lay	1	Onion, French	1
Bleu cheese	1	Tabouli (bulgur wheat), seasoned	2
Clam	1		
Enchilada, Frito-Lay	1		
Garlic	1	Tasty Tartar, Borden	1
Green Goddess	1	Western Bar B-Q, Borden	1
Guacamole, 1/4 cup	2		

GRAINS

Grains come in different packages. What they share is that they are cereal seeds. The Cancer Institute tells us we should choose whole grains (whole seeds) over crushed grains, such as flour, to keep us on the path of most resistance to cancer.

You'll find the Grain category broken into various subcategories that will make it easy for you to look up the foods you are searching for when you want to know their unit values. The categories that follow are Breads, Cereals, Crackers, Muffins, Rolls, and Miscellaneous Grains.

BREADS

(1 ounce unless noted)	WWUS
Banana nut	2
Banana tea	2
Boston brown	2
Bran raisin	2
Breadsticks, 2	1
Cheese, party, Pepperidge Farm	1
Cinnamon	1
Cinnamon raisin	1
Corn & Molasses, Pepperidge Farm	1
Cornbread, 3 cubic inches	1
Corn pone, 1 cake	2
Cracked wheat	1
Date nut	2
Egg sesame	2
French	1
Fresh Horizons, light and dark	1
Garlic bread	2
Glutogen Gluten, Thomas'	1
Hillbilly	1
Hollywood, light and dark	1
Honey bran	1
Honey cracked wheat	1

	WWUS
Honey Wheat Berry, Pepperidge Farm	1
Italian	1
King's Bread, Wasa	4
Natural Health, Arnold	1
Oatmeal	1
Panettone, wine fruit loaf	2
Pita bread, white or whole wheat	1
Profile, light and dark	1
Protogen Protein, Thomas'	1
Pumpernickel	1
Pumpernickel party, 2 slices	1
Raisin	1
Rite Diet, Thomas'	1
Roman Meal	1
Rye	1
Rye pumpernickel	1
Salt-free	1
Salt-rising	1
Slender Key, Arnold	1
Soft sandwich	1
Spoonbread	3
Vienna	1
Wheat-Germ, Pepperidge Farm	1

	WWUS
White bread	1
Whole wheat	1

CEREALS

(1 cup unless noted)
Cold, Ready-to-Eat

	WWUS
All-Bran, Kellogg's	2
Alpen	3
Alpha-Bits	2
Apple Jacks	2
Boo Berry, 1 ounce	2
Bran, 100%, Nabisco	2
Bran Buds, Kellogg's	2
Bran Chex, Ralston, 2/3 cup	2
Bran Flakes, 40%	2
Bran Flakes, raisins, 1 ounce	2
Buc Wheats, 1 ounce	2
Cap'n Crunch, 1 ounce	2
Cap'n Crunchberries, 1 ounce	2
Cap'n Crunch Punch Crunch, 1 ounce	2
Cap'n Crunchberries Peanut Butter, 1 ounce	2
Cap'n Crunch Vanilly, 1 ounce	2
Charged Bran, Ralston	2
Cheerios	2
Cocoa Krispies	2

	WWUS
Cocoa Pebbles	2
Cocoa Puffs, 1 ounce	2
Concentrate, Kellogg's, 1/2 cup	3
Cookie Crisp, Chocolate Chip	2
Cookie Crisp, Vanilla Wafer	2
Corn Bran, 1 ounce	2
Corn Chex, Ralston	2
Corn Flakes	2
Corn Flakes, sugar-coated, 1 ounce	2
Corn Total, 1 ounce	2
Corny Snaps, Kellogg's, 1 ounce	2
Count Chocula, 1 ounce	2
Country Morning, Kellogg's, 1/2 cup	3
Country Morning, raisins and dates, 1/2 cup	3
Crispy Critters	2
Crispy Wheats 'n Raisins, 1 ounce	2
C.W. Post, 1/2 cup	4
C.W. Post with raisins, 1 ounce	2
Franken Berry, 1 ounce	4
Froot Loops	2
Frosted Flakes, Kellogg's	2

	WWUS		WWUS
Frosted Mini-Wheats, 4 pieces	2	Natural, 100% Quaker, 1 ounce	2
Frosted Rice, Kellogg's, 1 ounce	2	Natural, 100% Quaker, apples, cinnamon, 1 ounce	2
Frosted Rice Krinkles, Post	2	Natural, 100% Quaker, raisins, dates, 1 ounce	2
Frosty O's, General Mills, 1 ounce	2	Oat Flakes	2
Fruit and Bran, 1 ounce	2	Pep, Kellogg's	2
Fruit Brute, General Mills, 1 ounce	2	Product 19	2
Fruity Pebbles, Post	2	Puffa Puffa Rice, Kellogg's	2
Golden Grahams	2	Puffed Corn, sweetened, 1 ounce	2
Granola, 1 ounce	2		
Grape-Nut Flakes, 1 ounce	2	Puffed Oats, plain or sweetened, 1 ounce	2
Grape-Nuts, 1 ounce	2	Puffed Rice, 2 cups	2
Heartland Granola Puffs, 1/2 cup	2	Puffed Wheat, 2 cups	2
		Quisp, Quaker	2
Heartland Natural, 1 ounce	2	Raisin Bran, Kellogg's	2
		Raisin Bran, Post	3
Heartland Natural, raisins, 1 ounce	2	Rice Chex, 1 ounce	2
		Rice Flakes, 1 ounce	2
Honeycomb	2	Rice Krispies	2
Kaboom, General Mills, 1 ounce	2	Rice Toasties	2
		Shredded corn or rice, 1 ounce	2
King Vitaman, 1 ounce	2		
Kix	2	Shredded Wheat, 1 biscuit	2
Life	2		
Lucky Charms, 1 ounce	2	Shredded Wheat, spoon-size	3

	WWUS
Sir Grapefellow, 1 ounce	2
Special K	2
Sugar Pops	2
Sugar Snacks	2
Super Sugar Crisp	2
Team Flakes	2
Total, 1 ounce	2
Trix, 1 ounce	2
Wheat Chex	2
Wheat Flakes	2
Wheaties	2

Hot, Cooked

	WWUS
Bulgur, 1/2 cup	2
Cornmeal, cooked, 1/2 cup	1
Cream of Rice, 3/4 cup	2
Cream of Wheat, 3/4 cup	2
Farina, 1 cup	2
Grits, corn, 1 cup	2
Grits, hominy, 1 cup	2
Maltex, 3/4 cup	2
Maypo, 1 ounce, dry, any flavor	2
Oatmeal, 3/4 cup	2
Oatmeal, maple, brown sugar, 3/4 cup	3
Oatmeal with raisins and spice, 3/4 cup	2
Pep, Kellogg's, 1 cup	2
Ralston, 2/3 cup	2

	WWUS
Wheat Germ, 2 tablespoons	1

CRACKERS

	WWUS
American Harvest, 3	1
Arrowroot Biscuit, 2	1
Bacon-Flavored Thins, 5	1
Bacon Nips, 1 ounce	2
Bacon Rinds, 1 ounce	2
Butter Thins, 3	1
Cheese and Peanut Butter Sandwich, 2	1
Cheese Goldfish, Pepperidge Farm, 10	1
Cheese 'n Cracker, 1 package	2
Cheese Nips, Nabisco, 10	1
Cheese Pixies, 1-ounce bag	2
Cheese Tid-Bits, 10	1
Cheese Twists, 1 ounce	2
Chee·tos, 1 ounce	2
Cheez-It, Sunshine, 10	1
Cheez Waffles, Old London, 5	1
Chicken in a Biskit, Nabisco, 5	1
Chippers, 4	1
Chipsters, 20	1
Cinnamon Toast, Sunshine, 3	1

	WWUS		WWUS
Club Crackers, Keebler, 3	1	OTC (Original Trenton Crackers), 3	2
Craquottes, 4	1	Oysterettes, 20	1
Crown Pilot, 1	1	Peanut Butter, malted milk, 3	2
Escort, Nabisco, 3	1		
Goldfish, all kinds, 20	1	Peanut Butter sandwich, 1	2
Graham, 2½" square, 2	1		
		Pizza Spins, 32	2
Graham, chocolate or cocoa-covered, 2	2	Pizza Wheels, ¾-ounce bag	2
Graham, sugar-honey coated, 2	1	Potato Crisps, 16	2
		Rice Cakes, 2	1
Hi-Ho, Sunshine, 4	1	Rice Wafers, 6	1
Matzo, egg, 1	2	Ritz, Nabisco, 3	1
Matzo, Egg 'n Onion, 1	2	Ritz Cheese, Nabisco, 6	1
Matzo, Midgetea, 1	1	Roman Meal Wafers, 3	1
Matzo, Onion Tams, 5	1	Rusk, 1	1
Matzo, regular, unsalted, ½ board	1	Rye Thins, 5	1
		Rye Toast, 5	1
Matzo, Round Tea, 1	1	Rye Wafers, 3	1
Matzo, Tam Tams, 5	1	Rye Wafers, whole grain, 2	1
Matzo, Tasteas, 1	2		
Matzo, Thin tea, 1	2	RyKrisp, plain and seasoned, 2 triple	1
Matzo, whole wheat, 1	2		
Melba Rounds, 5	1	Saltines, soda crackers, regular, unsalted, 4	1
Melba toast, rectangles, 5	2		
		Sesame, Ak-Mak, 1 ounce	1
Milk Lunch, Royal Lunch, 2	2		
		Sociables, Nabisco, 5	1
Norwegian Flatbread, 4	2	Swedish rye wafer, 10	1
Onion Rings, Wonder, 1 ounce	2	Town House, Keebler, 3	1

	WWUS		WWUS
Triangle Thins, Nabisco, 6	1	English	2
Triscuit, 3	1	English, buttered, McDonald's	3
Vegetable Thins, Nabisco, 4	1	Golden Egg Toasting, Arnold	2
Uneeda Biscuit, 2	1	Plain, home recipe	2
Wafer-ets, Hol-Grain, rice, 4	1	Raisin round, 2″ × 3″	3
Wafer-ets, Hol-Grain, wheat, 8	1	Scone	2
		Sourdough, 2 ounces	2
Waldorf, Keebler, 3	1	Soy, medium	2
Wasa Brod, 3	2	Wheat Berry, Wonder, 2 ounces	2
Waverly crackers, Nabisco, 3	1		

ROLLS
(1 unless noted)

Wheat Chips, General Mills, 8	1	Bagel	3
Wheat Thins, Nabisco, 6	1	Baking powder biscuit	2
		Barbecue, Arnold	2
Wheat Toast, Keebler, 3	1	Brown and serve	1
White Thins, Pepperidge Farm, 12	1	Butter Crescent, Pepperidge Farm	2
		Buttermilk biscuit	2
Whole wheat, 4	1	Cinnamon nut	2
Zwieback, 2	1	Cloverleaf roll	2
		Croissant	4

MUFFINS
(1 unless noted)

Blueberry, 3″ diameter	2	Dinner roll	1
Bran, 3″ diameter	2	Finger roll	1
Bran, Dunkin' Donuts	4	Frankfurter or hot dog roll	2
Cherry, Chef Francisco, average	2	Hamburger roll	2
		Hard, round or rectangular	2
Corn, 2 ounces	3	Kaiser roll	2

	WWUS		WWUS
Parkerhouse rolls	2	Flour, Softasilk, 1 cup	5
Pecan roll	4	Flour, wheat, all-purpose, sifted, 1/2 cup	3
Popover, 2 3/4" diameter at top	2		
Pumpernickel	3	Flour, wheat, all-purpose, unsifted, 1/2 cup	3
Raisin	3		
Rye	3		
Whole wheat	2	Flour, wheat, cake, sifted, unsalted, 1/2 cup	3

MISCELLANEOUS GRAINS

	WWUS		WWUS
Barley, pearled, regular and light, 1/2 cup	4	Flour, wheat, gluten, 1/2 cup	3
Bread crumbs, 1 ounce	2	Flour, wheat, self-rising, 1/2 cup	3
Corn fritter, 2" × 1 1/2"	2		
Cornmeal, bolted, cooked, 1 cup	2	Flour, whole wheat, 1 ounce	2
Cornmeal, bolted, dry, 1 cup	7	Matzo meal, 1/2 cup	3
Cornstarch, 2 tablespoons	1	Pancake, blueberry, 4" diameter, 1	2
Cracker crumbs, 1/2 cup	3	Pancake, buckwheat, 1 average	2
Cracker crumbs, graham, 1 cup	6	Pancake, buttermilk, 4" diameter, 1	2
Flour, buckwheat, 1 cup	4	Pancake, griddle cake, 4" diameter, 1	1
Flour, carob or St. John's, 1 ounce	1	Taco, 2 shells, 6" diameter	1
Flour, corn, 1/2 cup	3	Tortilla, corn, fried, 1 average	2
Flour, potato, 1 ounce	2		
Flour, rice, 1/2 cup	3	Tortilla, corn, yellow and white, 6" diameter, 1	1
Flour, rye, sifted, unsifted, 1/2 cup	3		

	WWUS		WWUS
Tortilla, corn, yellow and white, refined, 6" diameter, 1	2	Waffle, home recipe, 7" round, 1	3
Waffle, frozen, 4⁵/₈" × 3³/₄", 1	2	Wheat germ, 2 tablespoons	1
Waffle, frozen, blueberry or buttermilk, 1 medium	2		

SOUPS

(1 cup unless noted)

	WWUS		WWUS
Asparagus, cream of, made with milk	3	Beef noodle, Cup-a-Soup, 1 package	1
Asparagus, cream of, made with water	2	Beef noodle, with dumplings	2
Bean, black	2	Beef Sirloin Burger, Chunky	2
Bean curd	2	Borscht	2
Bean, homemade	3	Celery, cream of, made with water or milk	2
Bean, lima	2	Chicken, Chunky	2
Bean with pork, made with water	2	Chicken, cream of, Cup-a-Soup, 1 package	2
Bean with smoked ham	3	Chicken, cream of, made with.milk	3
Beef	2	Chicken, cream of, made with water	2
Beef, barley	2	Chicken and rice	1
Beef, chunky	3	Chicken broth, canned	1
Beef bouillon, 1 cube	0		
Beef bouillon, canned	1		
Beef-flavored, Cup-a-Soup, 1 package	1		

	WWUS		WWUS
Chicken Creole	2	Oyster stew, home recipe	3
Chicken gumbo	1		
Chicken noodle	1	Oyster stew, made with milk	3
Chicken vegetable	2		
Chicken vegetable, Cup-a-Soup, 1 package	1	Oyster stew, made with water	2
		Pea, Cup-a-Soup, 1 package	2
Chowder, clam, Manhattan-style	2		
		Pea, split	2
Chowder, clam, New England-style	3	Pea, split, with ham	2
		Pepper pot	2
Chowder, corn, New England-style	2	Potato, cream of, made with milk	3
Chowder, fish, New England-style	2	Potato, cream of, made with water	2
Egg drop	1	Shrimp, cream of, made with milk	3
Escarole and rice	3		
Frankfurter-bacon	4	Shrimp, cream of, made with water	2
Hot and sour	2		
Lentil	4	Subgum	2
Minestrone	3	Tomato, made with milk	2
Mulligatawny, homemade	2		
		Tomato, made with water	2
Mushroom, cream of, made with milk	3		
		Tomato beef	2
Mushroom, cream of, made with water	2	Tomato bisque	2
		Tomato rice	2
Mussel, Italian-style	5	Turkey, Chunky	2
Onion	2	Turkey noodle	2
Onion with 1 slice bread, topped with 2 ounces cheese	5	Turkey vegetable	2
		Vegetable, vegetarian	2
		Vegetable beef	2

	WWUS		WWUS
Vegetable with beef broth	2	Vichyssoise, canned	2
		Wonton	3

SNACKS

In the Snack category you will find candy and gum, crunchies, and nuts.

CANDY AND GUM

(1 ounce unless noted)	WWUS		WWUS
Almond, Toffee bar, Kraft	2	Caramel, vanilla with nuts	2
Almond Cluster	2	Caravelle	2
Almonds, chocolate-coated	2	Carmallow, 1 piece	2
Almonds, Jordan	2	Cashew Cluster, Kraft	2
Baby Ruth	2	Charleston Chew, ¾-ounce bar	2
Bit-O-Honey	2	Charleston Chew, bite-size, 2 pieces	1
Black Crows	2	Charms	2
Bonomo Turkish Taffy	2	Cherry, chocolate-covered, 2 pieces	2
Boston Baked Beans	2	Chewees, Curtiss	2
Bridge mix	2	Chocolate bar, bittersweet	2
Butterfinger, Curtiss	2	Chocolate bar, milk chocolate, Ghirardelli	2
Butterscotch	2		
Butterscotch morsels, Nestlé	2	Chocolate bar, milk chocolate, Hershey's	2
Candy corn	2	Chocolate bar, mint chocolate, Ghirardelli	2
Caramel, chocolate	2		
Caramel, chocolate-flavored roll	2	Chocolate bar, semisweet	2
Caramel, chocolate with nuts	2		
Caramel, vanilla	2		

	WWUS		WWUS
Chocolate bar, Special Dark, Hershey's	2	Clark	2
		Cluster, crispy	2
Chocolate-coated coconut center	2	Cluster, peanut, chocolate-covered	2
Chocolate-coated fudge	2	Coco-Mello, Nabisco, 1 piece	2
Chocolate-coated fudge with caramel and peanuts	2	Coconut bar, Curtiss	2
Chocolate-coated fudge with nuts	2	Coconut Bon Bons, Brach's, 1 piece	2
Chocolate-coated honeycomb hard candy with peanut butter	2	Coconut cream egg	2
		Coconut neapolitan, 1 piece	1
Chocolate-coated mints, 2½" × ⅜"	2	Coconut Squares, Nabisco, 1 piece	1
Chocolate-coated nougat and caramel	2	Coffee-ets, Saylor's, 4 pieces	1
Chocolate-coated peanuts	2	Coffee Nips, 2 pieces	1
Chocolate-coated raisins	2	Cup-O-Gold, Hoffman, 1 piece	3
Chocolate-coated vanilla cream	2	Dots, Mason	2
Chocolate parfait, 2 pieces	2	Eggs, Chuckles, 5 pieces	1
Choc-shop, Hoffman, 1 piece	3	Fiddle Faddle, 1½-ounce packet	3
Chuckles	2	Fifth Avenue	2
Chunky	2	Forever Yours	2
Circlets, Curtiss	2	Frappe, Welch's	2
Circus peanuts, Brach's, 2 pieces	1	Fruit 'n Nut, Nestlé's	2
		Fudge, chocolate, plain or with nuts, 1 cubic inch	2

	WWUS		WWUS
Fudge, vanilla, plain or with nuts, 1 cubic inch	2	Kisses, chocolate, Hershey's, 3 pieces	2
Fudge Bar, Welch's	2	KitKat	3
Fudge Nut Bar, Nabisco	2	Kraft caramels	2
Goobers	2	Licorice, Chuckles, 1	1
Good 'n Plenty	2	Licorice, Diamond Drops, Heide	2
Gum, Chiclets-type, 1 piece	0	Licorice, Pastilles, Heide	2
Gum, Chiclets-type, 8 pieces	1	Licorice, Switzer, red or black	2
Gum, stick, regular, 1 piece	0	Licorice, twist, red or black, 2 pieces	1
Gum, stick, regular, 8 pieces	1	Life Savers, drop or mint, 1 roll	2
Gum, stick, sugar-free, 1 piece	0	Lozenges, mint or wintergreen, Brach's, 4 pieces	1
Gum, stick, sugar-free, 8 pieces	1	Mallo Cup, Boyer	2
Hard candy, all kinds	2	Malted milk balls, chocolate-covered, 5 pieces	1
Heath English Toffee	2		
Hershey's Almond	2	Malted Milk Crunch, Welch's, 6 pieces	1
Hershey's Krackel	2		
Iced Jelly Cones, Brach's, 4 pieces	1	M&M's, plain and peanut	2
Jelly beans	2	Marathon	2
Jelly beans, Big Ben Jellies, 3 pieces	2	Mars Almond bar	2
		Marshmallows, 4 large	2
Jube Jels, Brach's, 4 pieces	1	Marshmallow, mini, 1/2 cup	2
Jujubes, 3 pieces	1		
Jujyfruits, Heide, 1 ounce	2	Mary Jane	2

	WWUS		WWUS
Mason Crows and Dots	2	Powerhouse	2
Milk Duds	2	Raisinets	2
Milk Shake, Hollywood	2	Red Hot Dollars	2
Milky Way	2	Red Hots	2
Mints, butter, 6 pieces	1	Saf-T Pops, Curtiss	2
Mints, chocolate-covered	2	Snickers	2
		Spearmint leaves, 3 pieces	2
Mints, dessert, 10 pieces	1	Sprigs	2
		Sprint	2
Mints or Peppermints, after-dinner, all kinds	2	Stars, chocolate, 3 pieces	1
		Sugar Babies, 12	2
Mr. Goodbar	2	Sugar Daddy, giant sucker	23
Mounds	2		
Necco Canada Mints, all flavors, 3 pieces	1	Sugar Daddy, junior sucker, plain or chocolate	1
Necco Wafers, 12 pieces	1		
		Sugar Daddy, nugget, 2 pieces	1
Nestlé's Crunch	2		
Nibs	2	Sugar Daddy, sucker, caramel	2
Oh Henry!	2		
$100,000 bar	2	Sugar Mama	2
Orange slices	2	Sugar Wafer	2
Payday, Hollywood	2	Taffy, saltwater, 2 pieces	1
Peanut bars	2		
Peanut brittle	2	Taffy, Turkish	2
Peanut Butter Cups, Boyer	3	3 Musketeers	2
		Tic Tacs, 15	1
Peanut Butter Cups, Reese's	2	Toffee, all flavors, 2 pieces	1
Pom Poms, 12	3	Tootsie Roll	2
Poppycock	2	Tootsie Roll Pop	1

	WWUS		WWUS
Tootsie Roll Pop-drop, 3 pieces	1	Popcorn, air-popped, 3 cups	1
Triple Decker Bar, Nestlé's	2	Popcorn, caramel, 3/4-ounce bag	3
CRUNCHIES		Popcorn, cheese-flavored, 3/4-ounce bag	3
(1 ounce unless noted)		Popcorn, regular, plain, 2 cups	1
Bacon Nips, Frito-Lay	2	Potato chips, all brands	2
Bacon Rinds, Wonder	2	Potato Crisps	2
Bacon Tasters, Old London	2	Potato sticks	2
Banana Chips	2	Pretzels, Dutch, 1 piece	1
Bugles	2	Pretzels, logs, 2	1
Cheese Puffs	2	Pretzels, nuggets	2
Chee·tos	2	Pretzels, pretzelettes, 5 pieces	1
Chipsters	2	Pretzels, ring	2
Chow Mein noodles	2	Pretzels, rods	2
Clam-flavored Crisps	2	Pretzels, 3-ring	2
Corn chips	2	Pretzel sticks, 20 pieces	1
Corn chips, barbecue flavor	2	Pretzel Twists	2
Corn chips, Nacho cheese flavor	2	Tortilla chips	2
Corn chips, Taco flavor	2	Tortilla chips, Piñata	2
Corn Diggers	2	NUTS	
Dipsy Doodles	2	Almond paste, 1 ounce	2
Doo Dads, 25 pieces	1	Almonds, in shell, 12	1
Flings, cheese-flavored	2	Almonds, roasted, 1 ounce	2
Flings, Swiss-'n-ham flavored	2	Almonds, shelled, chopped, 1 tablespoon	1
Funyums	2		
Hot Potatas	2		
Munchos	2		

	WWUS		WWUS
Almonds, slivered, 1 ounce	2	Peanuts, raw, 1 ounce	2
Beechnuts, 1 ounce	2	Peanuts, roasted, 1 tablespoon	2
Brazil nuts, 4–5 large	2	Peanuts, Spanish-type, 25	1
Brazil nuts, shelled, 1/3 cup	8		
Brazil nuts, unshelled, 8–9	4	Pecans, chopped, 1 tablespoon	1
Butternuts, 4–5	2	Pecans, large, 10	3
Cashews, roasted, 6–8	2	Pili nuts, 2 tablespoons	2
Cashews, roasted, 1 cup	8	Pine nuts (pignoli), shelled, 1 ounce	2
Chestnuts, 10	2	Piñon nuts, 2 tablespoons	2
Chestnuts, dried, 1 cup	4		
Chestnuts, fresh, 1/2 cup	3	Pistachio nuts, unshelled, 30 nuts	2
Coconut, dried, shredded, 1/2 cup	2	Pumpkin seeds, dry, hulled, 1 ounce	2
Coconut, fresh, shredded, 1/2 cup	2	Safflower seed kernels, 1 ounce	3
Coconut, fresh meat, 1" × 1" × 1/2" piece	1	Sesame seeds, dry, hulled, 1 tablespoon	1
Filberts, 10–12	2	Soybean nuts, 1 ounce	2
Hazelnuts, 10–12	2	Squash kernels, 1 ounce	2
Hickory nuts, 15 small	2		
Lichee nuts, dried, 6	1	Sunflower seeds, shelled, 1/2 ounce	1
Macadamia nuts, roasted, 6 whole	2		
Mixed nuts, shelled, 8–12	2	Walnuts, black, 8–10 halves	2
Peanuts, chopped, 1 tablespoon	1	Walnuts, English, 8–15 halves	2

JAMS, JELLIES, SWEETS, AND SYRUPS

(1 tablespoon unless noted)

	WWUS		WWUS
Apple butter	1	Malt, dry, 1 ounce	2
Chocolate, baking, 1 ounce	2	Malted milk, dry powder	2
Chutney, apple, 5 tablespoons	3	Marmalade, all varieties	1
Chutney, tomato, 5 tablespoons	2	Molasses, cane, Barbados, or blackstrap	1
Citron, 1 ounce	2		
Cocoa, plain, 2 tablespoons	1	Preserves, all varieties	1
Cocoa mix, 1 ounce	2	Sugar, brown, crude, 3 tablespoons	1
Gelatin, unflavored, 1 envelope	0	Sugar, brown, dark	1
Gelatin, unflavored, 3 envelopes	1	Sugar, confectioner's	1
		Sugar, corn, unrefined	1
Ginger, candied, 1 ounce	2	Sugar, maple, 1¼″ × 1″ × ½″	1
Grapefruit, lemon, or orange peel, candied, 1 ounce	2	Sugar, powdered	1
		Sugar, white, Domino, 2 cubes	1
Guava butter	1	Sugar, white, granulated	1
Honey	1	Sugarcane juice, 3 tablespoons	1
Jam, all varieties	1		
Jam, low-calorie, all varieties, 2 tablespoons	1	Syrup, cane, light	1
		Syrup, chocolate, fudge	1
Jelly, all varieties	1	Syrup, chocolate, low-calorie, 5 tablespoons	1
Jelly, low-calorie, all varieties, 2 tablespoons	1	Syrup, chocolate, thin-type	1
		Syrup, maple	1

	WWUS		WWUS
Syrup, sorghum	1	Topping, pecan, 1 ounce	2
Topping, butterscotch, 1 ounce	2	Topping, pineapple, 1 ounce	2
Topping, chocolate	1	Topping, strawberry, 1 ounce	2
Topping, fudge, 1 ounce	2		
Topping, hard sauce, 1/4 cup	3	Topping, walnut in syrup	1
Topping, marshmallow, 1 ounce	2	Topping, whipped, nondairy, 3 tablespoons	1
Topping, milk chocolate	1		

DRESSINGS, OILS AND FATS, AND SALADS

DRESSINGS

(1 tablespoon unless noted) WWUS

	WWUS		WWUS
Bleu/Roquefort	2	Hawaiian, Lowry's	2
Bleu/Roquefort, low-calorie	1	Herb and garlic	2
Caesar	1	Italian	2
Caesar, low-calorie	1	Italian, creamy	2
Canadian, Lawry's	1	Italian, low-calorie	1
Coleslaw	1	Mayonnaise	2
Coleslaw, low-calorie	1	Miracle Whip, Kraft	2
French	1	Oil and vinegar	2
French, homemade	2	Ranch-style, made with mayonnaise	1
French, low-calorie	1		
Fruit, Kraft	1	Rémoulade, Tillie Lewis	1
Garlic	1		
Green Goddess	1	Romano Caesar	2
Green Goddess, low-calorie	1	Russian	2
		Russian, low-calorie	1

	WWUS		WWUS
Salad dressing, mayonnaise or sour cream type	2	Spry	1
		Spry, light	1
		Suet	1
Sandwich spread	2	Vegetable oil	1
Sweet and sour, Kraft	1	Vegetable shortening	1
Thousand Island	2		

SALADS

(1/2 cup unless noted)

Thousand Island, low-calorie	1		
Tomato 'n Bacon	2	Apple, celery, and walnut salad	3
Tomato 'n Spice	2		
Vinaigrette	1	Cabbage salad, no dressing	0

OILS AND FATS

(2 teaspoons unless noted)

		Carrot and raisin salad	3
Bacon fat	1	Chef's salad, 1 ounce each, turkey, ham, and cheese, plain	4
Butter	1		
Butter, whipped, 1 tablespoon	1		
Chicken fat	1	Chicken salad	2
Cream substitutes, Coffee-mate, 2 tablespoons	1	Chicken with celery salad	3
Crisco shortening	1	Coleslaw with commercial French dressing	2
Fluffo shortening	1		
Lard	1		
Margarine	1	Coleslaw with homemade French dressing	2
Margarine, low-calorie, 1 tablespoon	1		
Margarine, whipped, 1 tablespoon	1	Coleslaw with mayonnaise	2
Olive oil	1	Coleslaw with mayonnaise-type salad dressing	1
Primex shortening	1	Crab salad	2
Salad oil	1	Egg salad	4
		Garden salad, plain	0

	WWUS		WWUS
Gelatin mold salad, 1/2 cup	2	Shrimp salad	2
Greek salad, 2 ounces feta cheese, plain	3	Spinach and bacon salad	2
Ham salad, 1 ounce	1	Spinach salad, plain	0
Lobster salad	2	Tabouli, 1 ounce	2
Macaroni salad	2	Tomato salad, jellied	1
Potato salad with mayonnaise	3	Tuna salad	2
Potato salad with salad dressing	2	Waldorf salad, 1 serving	2

SAUCES AND GRAVIES

(1/2 cup unless noted)

	WWUS		WWUS
Beef gravy, canned, Franco-American	2	Hollandaise sauce, mock	5
Brown gravy, homemade	4	Italian sauce	2
		Italian sauce with meat	2
Brown gravy, prepared, Durkee	1	Italian sauce with meatballs	3
Cheese sauce	4	Italian sauce with mushrooms	2
Chicken gravy, canned	2		
Chicken gravy, homemade	3	Marinara sauce	2
		Onion gravy, prepared, Kraft	1
Clam sauce, red	2		
Clam sauce, white	2	Sour cream sauce	4
Creole sauce	2	Spanish sauce	2
Enchilada sauce	1	Turkey gravy, homemade	3
Hard sauce	7		
Hollandaise sauce	5	Turkey gravy, prepared, French's	1

	WWUS		WWUS
White sauce, medium	3	White sauce, thin	2
White sauce, thick	3		

CONDIMENTS AND RELISHES

(1 tablespoon unless noted)

	WWUS		WWUS
A-1 Steak Sauce	0	Pickles, cucumber, bread and butter, 8 slices	1
A-1 Steak Sauce, 3 tablespoons	1		
Angostura Aromatic Bitters	1	Pickles, cucumber, dill, 1 large	0
Barbecue sauce, 3 tablespoons	1	Pickles, cucumber, sour, 1 large	0
Capers	0	Pickles, cucumber, sticks, candied, 4", 1	1
Catsup, 3 tablespoons	1	Pickles, cucumber, sweet, 1 large	2
Cauliflower, sweet, 2 buds	1		
		Pimientos	0
Chili sauce, 3 tablespoons	1	Relish, barbecue, 2 tablespoons	1
Horseradish, prepared	0	Relish, corn, 3 tablespoons	1
Mustard, brown and yellow	0	Relish, hamburger, 2 tablespoons	1
Olives, Greek-style, 1	2	Relish, hot dog	1
Olives, pitted, green, 10 giant	2	Relish, hot pepper	1
Onions, cocktail	0	Relish, Indian	1
Peppers, chile, pickled, hot, mild, sweet	0	Relish, piccalilli	1
		Relish, picnic	1
Pickles, chow-chow, sour, sweet, 1 ounce	1	Relish, sweet	1
		Soy sauce	0

	WWUS		WWUS
Steak sauce, 3 tablespoons	1	Tomato sauce, 1/2 cup	1
Sweet-and-sour sauce, 1 ounce	1	Vinegar, plain	0
Tabasco sauce	0	Vinegar, wine or flavored	0
Tartar sauce	2	Watermelon rind	1
Teriyaki sauce, 2 ounces, Kikkoman	1	Worcestershire Sauce	0
Tomato paste, 1/2 cup	2	Yeast, dry or Brewer's, 1 ounce	2

CHAPTER 8

The Main Event: Entrées, Vegetables, and Fruits

Let's take a minute to discuss entrées and their WWU values. There are entrées . . . and then there are *entrées:* plain broiled chicken or spinach and feta cheese pie! As the range of choices is very large, so are the WWU values. And remember—*where* you eat the particular entrée is important. There is usually a calorie difference between what you eat at home and what you eat out. Foods cost more in calories when they're served to you!

At home you can figure the WWUs just as we have done in this book. List all the ingredients for the particular dish, figure the calories from a calorie book, or use the food lists in this book. Remember, each Wild Weekend Unit contains about 75 calories. Total the calories, divide by the number of servings, and assign a WWU value to each serving. A recipe totaling 1,600 calories, which serves 4, gives a 400-calorie serving, which converts to 5 WWUs for each person per portion.

At the restaurant, alas, it's usually another story. We continue to caution that you must depend upon all your senses. Take a hard look. Is it 6 ounces of cooked meat, fish, or poultry, or is it more? How much butter or oil is on or in it? If you even suspect that this food is more fattening than home-cooked, you're probably right. So add more WWUs.

Without putting each ounce of meat into a calorimeter, thereby burning it up and making it unfit to eat, it is virtually impossible to know its caloric value. This is because the amount of fat in the meat, which may not be visible to your eye, can cause a wide swing in the number of calories. Standard sources of caloric values differ from one another. Even within U.S. Government publications there are variations, in different books, in the number of calories ascribed to the same food. The caloric values of the food that follow are an approximation based on information from standard government sources.

ENTRÉES

MEAT, POULTRY, AND FISH

BEEF AND BEEF DISHES

	WWUS
(6 ounces cooked, unless noted)	WWUS
Arm/blade, marbled, pot-roasted, 2 slices	3
Beefaroni, canned, 1 cup	3
Beef bourguignon	8
Beef Burgundy	3
Beef in barbecue sauce, frozen, 3/4 cup	3
Beef Stroganoff	8
Brisket, braised	9
Chipped beef with cream sauce and noodles, 1/2 cup	8
Chuck, ground	8
Chuck, lean	7
Club steak	6
Corned beef, canned	5
Corned beef, medium fat	10
Cubed steak	6
Dried beef, chopped	4
Dried beef, creamed, 1/2 cup	3
Eggplant and beef, Mrs. Paul's, 12-ounce package	5
Flank steak	7
Frankfurter, all beef, 4 (6 1/2 ounces)	7
Frozen beef dinner, 11-ounce size	5
Goulash, canned, 4 ounces	2
Hamburger patty	4
Meatballs, homemade	6
Meatballs, Italian, Invisible Chef, plain	3
Meat loaf, homemade	4

	WWUS		WWUS
Porterhouse steak, lean only	5	Chicken, dark and light, skinless, fried	6
Pot pie, frozen, 4¼" diameter, 8 ounces	7	Chicken, dark and light, with skin, fried	13
Pot roast	7	Chicken dinner, frozen, Swanson, Hungry Man	10
Rib roast	10		
Salisbury steak, frozen, 7 ounces	4	Chicken dinner, frozen, Swanson, 3-course 15-ounce dinner	8
Shepherd's pie	13		
Short ribs	10		
Sirloin, ground	9		
Sirloin, lean only	9	Chicken and dumplings, College Inn, canned, 5 ounces	3
Steak, chicken-fried	8		
Steak teriyaki	12		
Stew, frozen, 2-pound package	9	Chicken frankfurters, Weaver, 4	7
Stew, homemade, 1 cup	3	Chicken fricassee, homemade, 1 cup	5
Swiss steak with gravy	13		
T-Bone	6	Chicken marsala, homemade, 6 ounces, cooked meat	14
Tenderloin	6		

CHICKEN

(6 ounces cooked unless noted)

	WWUS		WWUS
		Chicken pot pie, homemade, 5½" with crust	15
Capon, with skin	7		
Chicken, canned, boned	4	Chicken ravioli, canned, 7 ounces	3
Chicken cordon bleu	15		
Chicken, dark and light, skinless	4	Chicken spread, canned, Underwood, 3 ounces	3
Chicken, dark and light, with skin	8	Chicken stew, canned, Swanson, 1 cup	2

	WWUS
Chicken stew, with dumplings, canned, Heinz, 8½-ounce can	3
Chicken tamale pie, Lynden Farms, canned, with sauce, ½ pie	2

FISH

(6 ounces cooked unless noted)

	WWUS
Abalone, raw	2
Albacore, tuna, raw	4
Anchovy, flat, 4	1
Anchovy, pickled	4
Barracuda, raw	3
Bass, striped	5
Bluefish	4
Bonito, canned	6
Buffalofish, raw	3
Butterfish, raw	4
Carp, raw	3
Catfish, raw	3
Caviar, 2 tablespoons	1
Clam cake, Mrs. Paul's, 2½" cake	2
Clams, canned, chopped, drained	2
Clams, fried, 1 pint	8
Clams, raw, cherrystones, 2	1
Cod	2
Cod, dried, salted	3

	WWUS
Crab, canned	3
Crab, deviled	3
Crab, fresh, all kinds	2
Eel, raw	5
Eel, smoked	7
Fish cakes, homemade or commercial, 1 2-ounce cake	2
Fish loaf, homemade	3
Fish sticks, frozen, 10	5
Flounder	2
Grouper, raw, 6 ounces	2
Haddock	3
Haddock, fried, 3" × 3" × ½"	2
Hake (whiting), raw, 6 ounces	2
Halibut, raw, 6 ounces	3
Herring, canned, in cream sauce, Vita, 8-ounce jar	5
Herring, kippered	4
Herring, pickled	5
Kingfish	3
Lobster	2
Lox, 1 ounce	1
Mackerel	3
Mackerel, canned, ½ cup	3
Mackerel, salted	7
Mackerel, smoked	5
Mullet, striped, breaded, fried	7

	WWUS		WWUS
Mussels, 1 ounce	1	Snails, raw, 6 ounces	2
Ocean Perch, raw, 6 ounces	2	Sole	2
		Sole Véronique	12
Octopus, raw, 6 ounces	2	Squid, raw, 6 ounces	2
Oysters, fried, 4 ounces	4	Sturgeon, smoked	3
Oysters, medium, 6–10	2	Swordfish	3
Oysters, scalloped, 6	4	Trout, brook, raw, 6 ounces	3
Oysters, smoked, Japanese baby, canned, 3²/₃ ounces	3	Trout, rainbow, raw, 6 ounces	4
Perch, fried	5	Tuna, canned in oil, 6 ounces	4
Pickerel, raw, 6 ounces	2		
Pike, raw, 6 ounces	2	Tuna, canned in water, 6 ounces	3
Pollack, cooked, creamed	3	Turtle, green, raw, 6 ounces	2
Pollack, raw, 6 ounces	2	Whitefish, baked	4
Pompano	7		
Red Snapper, raw	2	LAMB (lean only)	
Rockfish	3	*(6 ounces cooked unless noted)*	
Roe	4		
Sablefish, raw	4	Arm chop	5
Salmon, canned	4	Leg	5
Salmon, smoked	4	Loin chop	5
Salmon, steak	4	Rib chop	7
Sardines, canned, drained	4	Shoulder	4
Scallops	3	PORK	
Shad	4	*(6 ounces cooked unless noted)*	
Shrimp	3		
Shrimp, baked stuffed, 4 jumbo	17	Bacon, Canadian, ³/₄ ounce	1
Shrimp, fried	5	Bacon, cooked, 1 strip, 1 ounce uncooked	1
Smelt, 4–5 medium	2	Blade, marbled	8

	WWUS
Boston butt, marbled	8
Frankfurter, 4 (6½ ounces)	7
Ham, cured	6
Ham, fresh	8
Loin chop	8
Loin roast, lean only	6
Picnic, cured	7
Picnic shoulder, marbled	7
Sausage	
Blood, 1 link	3
Bockwurst	6
Cervelat, soft	7
Italian	3
Knockwurst	7
McDonald's, 1 patty	3
Pepperoni, Hormel	11
Mortadella	7
Polska, kielbasa, skinless, Eckrich	8
Scrapple	8
Brown 'n Serve	9
Vienna, link, bulk	10
Shoulder	7
Sirloin, marbled	7
Spareribs	7

POULTRY

(6 ounces cooked unless noted)

	WWUS
Duck, domesticated and wild, with skin	7
Duck, domesticated, skinless	4
Duck, wild, skinless	3
Goose, skinless	5
Goose, with skin	10
Hen and cock, light and dark, skinless	4
Pheasant, skinless	4
Quail, with skin	5
Rock cornish hen, with skin	4
Squab, pigeon, skinless	4
Squab, pigeon, with skin	8
Turkey, canned	4
Turkey, light and dark, skinless	4

VEAL

(6 ounces cooked unless noted)

	WWUS
Arm steak, lean and fat	7
Blade, lean and fat	7
Breast, stew meat, raw	8
Chop	8
Cutlet, breaded	7
Cutlet, round, lean only	7
Loin, medium fat	5
Sirloin, marbled	6
Steak	7

LUNCH MEATS	WWUS
(3 ounces unless noted)	
Barbecue loaf	2
Bologna, all beef, Oscar Mayer	3
Capicola	5
Ham, boiled or chopped	3
Ham, deviled, 1 tablespoon	1
Ham and cheese loaf, 3 slices	3
Headcheese	2
Honey loaf	2
Liver cheese	3
Liverwurst	5
Meat loaf	2
Old-fashioned loaf	2
Olive loaf	3
Pickle and pimiento loaf	3
Prem, 1 slice	4
Prosciutto	3
Salami, beef, Cotto	3
Salami, cooked	3
Salami, dry	4
Sandwich spread, Oscar Mayer, 1 slice	1
Spam, Hormel	3
Treet	3
Turkey roll, Swift	2

VARIETY MEATS	WWUS
(6 ounces boiled unless noted)	
Brains, all kinds, raw	3
Chitterlings	8
Giblets	
Chicken, fried	5
Turkey, simmered	5
Gizzards	
Chicken	3
Turkey	4
Heart	
Beef, braised	4
Calf, braised	4
Chicken, simmered	4
Turkey, simmered	4
Kidneys	
Beef	5
Calf, raw	3
Liver	
Beef, broiled	3
Beef, fried	5
Calf, fried	6
Calf, raw	3
Chicken	4
Chicken, simmered	4
Lamb, broiled	6
Turkey, simmered	4
Liver and onions, 1 restaurant serving, pan-fried	3
Stomach, pork, scalded	3

	WWUS		WWUS
Sweetbreads		Horsemeat, raw, 6 ounces	3
Beef	7	Lean strips with bacon flavor, General Foods	11
Calf	4		
Lamb, braised	4		
Tongue		Lentils, cooked, drained, 1/2 cup	2
Beef, braised	5		
Calf, braised	4	Peanut butter, 1 tablespoon	2
Tripe, beef	3		
Tripe, beef, pickled	2	Rabbit, domestic, baked	4

Other Proteins

(6 ounces broiled unless noted)

	WWUS		WWUS
Alligator meat	5	Rabbit, wild, raw, 6 ounces	3
Armadillo meat	4	Raccoon, roasted	5
Bean curd, firm, 6 ounces	3	Reindeer, raw, 6 ounces	5
Bean curd, soft, 6 ounces	2	Snail, raw	2
Beaver, roasted	5	Soybeans, dry, cooked, 1/2 cup	2
Breakfast links, Morning Star Farms, 1 piece	1	Soybeans, dry, raw, 1/2 cup	5
Chick peas, 1/4 cup	3	Tofu (soybean curd), firm, 6 ounces	3
Frog legs, fried	7	Tofu (soybean curd), soft, 6 ounces	2
Frog legs, raw, 6 ounces	2	Turtle, green, canned	3
Hare, raw, 6 ounces	3	Venison, roasted	3
		Whale meat, raw	3

EGGS AND EGG DISHES

	WWUS		WWUS
Egg McMuffin, McDonald's	4	Eggs, substitutes for	
		Egg Beaters,	2
Eggs, chicken		Fleischmann's, 1/4	
Boiled, hard or soft, whole, medium	2	cup	
		Eggstra, Tillie Lewis,	1
Omelet, plain, medium	2	1 serving	
		Eggs Benedict	7
Omelet, Spanish	4	Quiche, cheese,	3
Scrambled	2	homemade, 1/6th	
Whites, large, 3	1	Quiche, ham,	3
Yolk, large	1	homemade, 1/6th	
Eggs, other, whole, medium		Quiche Lorraine,	5
Duck	2	homemade, 1/6th	
Goose	2	Quiche, plain,	3
Quail	1	homemade, 1/6th	
Turkey	2	Quiche, vegetable,	3
Turtle	2	homemade, 1/6th	

PASTA

WWU values for pasta differ depending on whether the dish is homemade, canned, or restaurant-prepared.

For homemade, figure the calories as you would for any other dish according to the information at the start of this chapter.

The canned pasta WWU values are consistent. Measure carefully your correct portion. If you're eating pasta at home, you control the portion size. Count each cup of pasta as 2 WWUs. Add WWUs for the tomato sauce, cheese, and any meat in the dish.

In the restaurant, use your eyes. How much pasta is on your plate? A cup? Two cups? A kettleful? Allot 2 WWUs for each cup. Check the cheese and sauce. Is it a cup, a 1/2 cup, or the entire tomato garden? The WWUs below are based on an average restaurant portion unless otherwise noted.

	WWUS		WWUS
Alla ghiotta	14	Pasta with pesto sauce	12
Fettuccine Alfredo	5	Ravioli, beef	7
Lasagna	8	Ravioli, cheese	7
Linguine with white clam sauce	7	Spaghetti and meatballs in tomato sauce, 1 cup	4
Macaroni and beef, canned, 1 cup	3		
Macaroni and cheese, baked, homemade 1 cup	5	Spaghetti carbonara, 1 serving	12
Manicotti	10	Spaghetti in tomato sauce with cheese, 1 cup	3
Pasta with meat sauce	8		

FAST FOODS

(regular restaurant serving unless noted)

	WWUS		WWUS
Big Mac, McDonald's	7	Hot dog, deluxe, with cheese and bun	8
Cheeseburger with bun	4		
Chili dog with bun	4	Mariner platter, Burger Chef	9
Chili dog with cheese and bun	5	Rancher platter, Burger Chef	8
Fish sandwich with sauce and bun	5		
		Triple hamburger	11
Hamburger, 1/4 pound, with bun	5	Triple hamburger, with cheese and bun	13
Hamburger, 1/4 pound, with cheese and bun	7	Whaler, Burger King	8
		Whopper, Burger King	8

Fast Food Addendum: A positive aspect of all fast-food restaurants is that the portion sizes are uniform. A Big Mac in San Francisco is the same as a Big Mac in New York or Kalamazoo . . . and in your hometown. This consistency of size and calories applies to the items served in most other franchised fast-food restaurants as well.

FOREIGN CUISINES

AFRICAN

	WWUS		WWUS
Chicken with yoloff rice	13	Noodle stew	14
		Spinach stew	13
Ham kariba	16		
Nikatse nkwa (chicken in peanut sauce)	11		

BRITISH

	WWUS		WWUS
Cornish pastie, 1	13	Lancashire hot pie	6
Irish lamb stew	8	Steak and kidney pie	18

CHINESE

As with Italian food, Chinese comes in small, regular, large, and you-must-be-kidding portion sizes. Use your eyes to judge, then gauge WWUs accordingly. The WWUs below are figured on an average-size portion.

	WWUS		WWUS
Chicken chow mein	7	Chicken with snow peas	5
Chicken subgum	3		
Chicken with chestnuts	7	Chop suey with beef or pork	8
Chicken with peanuts or cashews	6	Egg foo yong, 1 patty with gravy	3

	WWUS		WWUS
Fried shrimp, 5	4	Stir-fried bean curd	2
Lobster Cantonese	15	and vegetables	
with pork		Stir-fried chicken	7
Moo goo gai pan	7	Stir-fried scallops	2
Pork lo mein	9	Striped bass with	5
Pork with broccoli	4	pungent sauce	
Spicy pork with bean	4	Sweet and sour pork	5
curd		Sweet and sour shrimp	4
Steamed chicken with	3	Tzuoijia (crispy fried	13
sausage		duck)	

FRENCH

The French are famous for their marvelous butter and cream sauces. Our WWUs are figured on an average preparation and serving size. If you detect a lot of butter add at least 3 WWUs. Use your senses!

Don't mistake *nouvelle cuisine* for low-caloric preparation. What it gives up in flour it makes up in butter and oil. You can give thanks, though, for the generally smaller portions.

	WWUS		WWUS
Auvergne leg of lamb	9	Poulet Basque	10
Beef bourguignon	8	Quenelles de prochet	7
Béarnaise vegetable	10	(Pike Quenelles)	
stew		Quiche aux	7
Bouillabaisse	6	champignons	
Marseillaise		(mushroom quiche)	
Braised rabbit	7	Sole Bretonne	4
Côtes de veau au	19	Stuffed pheasant	8
Calvados (veal chops		Veal fricassee	9
with apple brandy)			

GREEK

Beware of oil in Greek entrées. Greek food is wonderful but not slimming. If you taste oil add WWUs.

	WWUS		WWUS
Aegean calamari	7	Shish kebab	10
Chicken and pilaf casserole	10	Shrimp baked with feta, tomato, ouzo, and cognac	8
Eggplant moussaka	14		
Greek casserole	12		
Lamb stew	7	Spinach and feta pita, 1 pita	21
Paprika stew	8		
Roast leg of lamb with orzu	8	Stifado (beef stew with wine)	10

HUNGARIAN

	WWUS		WWUS
Hungarian goulash	9	Paprika veal	11
Paprika chicken	7		

INDIAN

Assess your entrée for extra sauces and add WWUs accordingly. The same applies for overly generous portions of Indian food.

	WWUS		WWUS
Ande ki kari (whole eggs in spicy tomato sauce)	3	Mughalai pullad (lamb pilaf)	14
Bhoni machi (fried filet of sole with carom)	8	Murgh masala (chicken in onion-tomato gravy)	8
Gosht do-piaza (meat smothered with onions)	8	Rogani gosht (braised lamb in cream sauce)	10
Gosht kari (meat curry)	9		
Masala jheen gari (shrimp laced with mild spices)	8	Shani murgh badaami (royal chicken in silky white almond sauce)	11

	WWUS		WWUS
Sookha keema (dry-cooked spicy ground lamb or beef)	7	Tandoori murghi (Indian barbecued chicken)	4
Tali machi (chick-pea battered fish)	7		

JEWISH STYLE

	WWUS		WWUS
Blintze, plain, homemade, 1/6th	3	Holishkes, homemade, 1/6th	5
Blintze, vegetable, homemade, 1/6th	4	Meat and carrot tzimmes, homemade, 1/8th	8
Cabbage soup, homemade, 1/10th	7	Noodle apple pudding, homemade, 1/8th	4
Chicken liver pie, homemade, 1/6th	3		

ITALIAN

(1 restaurant-size serving unless noted)

As we've hinted delicately before, there are Italian restaurants with small portions, and then there are those we know and love, with *enormous* portions. Remember that our WWU counts for Italian entrées, e.g., cheese ravioli, are based on the *average-size* restaurant portion. If you order cheese ravioli frequently in various restaurants, then you know what the average portion looks like. If the serving seems small, figure the standard WWU value anyway, to boost your weight loss, but if the portion is larger than usual, you must add more WWUs. You can kid yourself, but you can't kid your body. If the cheese ravioli (or anything else) is double the normal size, then it's double the normal WWUs. The laws of mathematics are not open to negotiation. The following WWU counts are based on one restaurant serving size unless noted.

	WWUS		WWUS
Baked polenta with pork	9	Pizza, pepperoni, 1/2 of 10" pie	6
Beef bracciole	5	Pizza, sausage, 1/8th of 9" pie	3
Cheese gnocchi with tomato sauce	12	Potato gnocchi with meat sauce	8
Chicken breasts with prosciutto and cheese	7	Risotto con salciccia	10
Chicken cacciatore	8	Saltimbocca	7
Eggplant parmigiana	7	Steak pizzaola	9
Pizza, anchovy, 1/2 of 10" pie	5	Veal cutlet	4
Pizza, cheese, 1/2 of 10" pie	6	Veal parmigiana	7
		Veal piccata	5
Pizza, mushroom, 1/8th of 9" pie	3	Veal scallopini	5
		Veal scallopini marsala	5

JAPANESE

(WWU count based on 6 ounces cooked protein, unless noted)

The WWU counts for the Japanese entrées are figured on average-size portions and plain (Cool List) food preparation methods. If you visit a Japanese restaurant where the food is oily or served in a sauce or gravy, add WWUs accordingly.

	WWUS		WWUS
Beef Sukiyaki	13	Mazezushi (vinegared rice mixed with vegetables and seafood)	3
Beef Teriyaki	10		
Chawan musni (chicken and shrimp in egg custard)	2		
		Miso-ni (Boston mackerel in miso sauce, 5 ounces cooked mackerel)	7
Kamo yoshino-ni (duck seasoned in sake-seasoned sauce)	10		

	WWUS		WWUS
Okaribayaki (pan-broiled duck and vegetable with dipping sauce)	16	Shabu shabu (beef and vegetables cooked in broth with dipping sauce)	8
Sakamushni (sake-steamed fish with tofu and spinach)	2	Sushi, 3 pieces	2
Sashimi (raw fish), 10 ounces	5	Tempura (deep-fried shrimp and vegetables in batter)	4
		Tori teriyaki (ginger chicken with a sweet, soy-seasoned glaze)	5

MEXICAN

(1 restaurant-size serving, unless noted)

It cannot be said too often—the WWU counts for any restaurant entrée are figured on the *average*-size serving. If your plate is heaped higher than usual, add more WWUs!

	WWUS		WWUS
Arroz con pollo	5	Enchilada, cheese, 1	5
Burrito, beef, 1	5	Enchilada, pork, 1	4
Burrito, chicken, 1	4	Enchirito	5
Burrito, pork, 1	7	Huevos Rancheros	8
Carne Asada	5	Pintos and cheese	3
Chalupas, 1	3	Quesadilla, 1	4
Chili, 1 cup	3	Taco, beef, 1	4
Chili con carne, 1 cup	3	Taco, pork, 1	4
Chili rellenos	4	Tamale, 1	3
Chimichanga, beef	5	Tortilla casserole	4
Chorizo, 1/2 cup	3	Tostada, beef	5

RUSSIAN

	WWUS		WWUS
Cabbage pastie, 1	7	Uzbek pilaf	14
Chicken caucasia	8		

VEGETABLES, LEGUMES, AND STARCHES

(1/2 cup cooked, unless noted)

	WWUS		WWUS
Alfalfa sprouts	0	Carrot tzimmes, home recipe	2
Artichoke	0		
Artichoke, marinated, drained, 5 hearts	1	Cauliflower	0
		Celery	0
Asparagus	0	Chick peas (garbanzo beans)	4
Avocado, puree (guacamole), 1/2 cup	3		
		Chives	0
Avocado, small, 1/4	1	Collard greens	0
Bamboo shoots	0	Corn, cream-style	2
Bean sprouts	0	Corn, sweet, fresh	1
Beans, baked, no pork	2	Corn on the cob, 4 ounces, 1 ear	2
Beans, green, snap	0		
Beans, kidney	2	Cucumber	0
Beans, lima	2	Daikon	0
Beans, navy	2	Eggplant	0
Beans, yellow	0	Endive	0
Beets	1	Garlic	0
Bok choy	0	Kale	0
Broccoli	0	Kohlrabi	0
Brussels sprouts	0	Leeks	1
Cabbage	0	Lentils	2
Cabbage, sweet and sour	2	Lettuce, all varieties	0
		Mushrooms	0
Carrot pudding	4	Mustard greens	0
Carrots	0	Okra	1

	WWUS		WWUS
Onions, cooked	1	Potato puffs, french-fried, 3 ounces	3
Onions, creamed	2		
Onions, raw	0	Pumpkin	1
Parsnip	1	Radishes	0
Peas, all varieties	1	Rhubarb	0
Peppers	0	Rice, brown or white, hot	1
Peppers, sweet-pickled	2		
Pimiento	0	Rice, curried	2
Potato, au gratin, escalloped, no cheese	3	Rice, fried	2
		Rice, Spanish	2
Potato, au gratin, escalloped with cheese	2	Rice, white, precooked instant	1
		Rice, wild, 1/3 cup	1
Potato, baked stuffed with cheese or sour cream and cheese	4	Rice pilaf	2
		Rutabaga	1
		Sauerkraut, unsweetened, canned	0
Potato, french-fried, 2″ × 1/2″ × 1/2″, 10 pieces	2	Spinach	0
		Squash, acorn, baked or boiled, mashed	1
Potato, hash-brown	3		
Potato, mashed, milk added	1	Squash, hubbard, baked or boiled, mashed	1
Potato, mashed, milk and butter added	2		
		Squash, spaghetti	0
Potato, pan-fried	3	Squash, summer	0
Potato, small, baked, or boiled	1	Squash, winter, baked or boiled, mashed	1
		String beans	0
Potato, Tiny-Taters, Bird's-Eye, 3 ounces	2	Succotash	2
		Sweet potatoes, 5″ × 2″	2
Potato kugel, 1/6th home recipe	3		
		Sweet potatoes, boiled, mashed	2
Potato latke, 2	3		

	wwus		wwus
Tomatoes, boiled	0	Tomato puree	1
Tomatoes, diced in puree	1	Turnip	0
		Water chestnuts, 4	1
Tomatoes, stewed	1	Watercress	0
Tomatoes, whole, medium, 1	0	Zucchini	0
		Zucchini, canned in tomato sauce	1
Tomato paste	2		

FRUITS

	wwus		wwus
Apple, baked, medium, with 2 tablespoons sugar	3	Apricots, water-pack, 3 medium halves	1
Apple, fresh, whole, large	2	Avocado, medium, 1/2	3
		Banana, large	2
Apple, fresh, whole, medium	1	Banana, medium	2
		Banana, small	1
Apple, fresh, whole, small	1	Banana flakes, 1/2 cup	3
		Blackberries, fresh or frozen, 1 cup	1
Applesauce, sweetened, 1/2 cup	2	Blueberries, fresh or frozen, 1 cup	1
Applesauce, unsweetened, 1/2 cup	1	Boysenberries, canned or fresh, 1 cup	1
Apricots, dried, uncooked, 3 halves	1	Boysenberries, unsweetened, frozen, 1 cup	1
Apricots, in heavy syrup, 3 medium halves	2	Cantaloupe, medium, 1/2	1
Apricots, juice-pack, 3 medium halves	1	Casaba melon, 2″ wedge	1
Apricots, 2–3 medium	1	Cherries, maraschino, 12 large	2

	WWUS		WWUS
Cherries, sour, fresh, 1/2 cup	1	Grapes, fresh, 1/2 cup	1
		Guava, medium	1
Cherries, sweet, fresh, 20 large	2	Honeydew melon, 1/4 small	1
Crab apples, fresh, 31/2 ounces	1	Kiwi, 2	1
		Kumquat, 5–6 medium	1
Cranberries, fresh or frozen, 1/2 cup	1	Lemon, whole	0
		Lichees, dried, 1 ounce	2
Cranberry sauce, 2 tablespoons	1	Lichees, fresh, 3 ounces	1
Currants, fresh, black or red, 1/2 cup	1	Lime, whole	0
		Loganberries, fresh, 1/2 cup	1
Dates, pitted, 8 medium	4	Loganberries, heavy syrup, 1/2 cup	2
Elderberries, fresh, 3 ounces	1	Loganberries, water-pack, 1/2 cup	1
Figs, dried or fresh, 1 small	1	Mango, fresh, 1/2 medium	1
Fruit cocktail, heavy syrup, 1/2 cup	2	Melon balls, fresh, 1/2 cup	1
Fruit cocktail, water-pack, 1/2 cup	1	Melon balls, sweetened, frozen, 1/2 cup	2
Gooseberries, fresh or water-pack, 1/2 cup	1	Melon balls, unsweetened, frozen, 1/2 cup	1
Gooseberries, heavy syrup, 1/2 cup	2	Mulberries, fresh, 1/2 cup	1
Grapefruit, fresh, pink or white, 1/2 medium	1	Nectarine, fresh, medium	1
Grapefruit, heavy syrup, 1/2 cup	2	Orange, mandarin, 1 cup	2
Grapefruit sections, water-pack, 1/2 cup	1		

	WWUS		WWUS
Orange, whole, fresh, large	2	Plums, syrup-pack, 1/2 cup	2
Orange, whole, fresh, medium	1	Pomegranate, fresh, medium	1
Orange, whole, fresh, small	1	Prunes, fresh, 4 large	2
Orange peel, raw	0	Prunes, sweet, cooked, 4 medium	3
Orange segments, 1/2 cup	1	Pumpkin, fresh or cooked, 1/2 cup	1
Papaya, fresh, 1/2 medium	1	Quince, fresh, 3 ounces	1
Peach, fresh, medium	1	Raisins, seedless, 4 tablespoons	2
Peaches, syrup-pack, 1/2 cup	2	Raspberries, black or red, fresh, 1/2 cup	1
Peaches, water-pack, 1/2 cup	1	Rhubarb, cooked, sweetened, 1/2 cup	2
Pear, fresh, medium	1	Rhubarb, fresh, uncooked, 1 cup	0
Pears, syrup-pack, 1/2 cup	2	Rhubarb, frozen, unsweetened, uncooked, 1/2 cup	1
Pears, water-pack, 1/2 cup	1	Strawberries, fresh or frozen, 1/2 cup or 10 large	1
Persimmon, medium	1		
Pineapple, fresh, 1/2 cup	1	Strawberries, frozen, sweetened, sliced, 1/2 cup	2
Pineapple, juice-pack, 1/2 cup	1		
Pineapple, syrup-pack, 1/2 cup	2	Strawberries, frozen, sweetened, whole, 1/2 cup	2
Pineapple, water-pack, 1/2 cup	0		
Plantain, fresh, small	1	Tangelo, fresh, medium	1
Plums, fresh, 2 medium	1	Tangerine, fresh, large	1

	WWUS		WWUS
Tomato, fresh, large	0	Watermelon, slice,	2
Watermelon, fresh, 1/2 cup	1	6″ × 1 1/2″	

CHAPTER 9

Grand Finale: Desserts, Dairy, and Beverages

WWU counting for the Dessert, Dairy, and Beverage categories is easy and straightforward. For beverages, the calories per portion are stated in any calorie list and these calories are easily converted to WWUs. For a mixed drink, we simply totaled the calories for each of the ingredients and assigned a WWU value in exactly the same way calories are determined for any recipe. That is, each WWU contains approximately 75 calories. For mixed drinks, we used the recipes in the Official Bartender's Guide.

The dessert count is derived in the same way—from calorie listings and cookbook recipe information.

WWU values for dairy products are figured directly from calorie lists and are probably the most reliable in this book. In the listing for dairy products we have included milk drinks, all kinds of milk, cream, yogurt, and cheese as well as imitation dairy products.

And so, there you have it. All previous cautions still hold when you eat away from home. To be diet-safe add a few WWUs. The sooner you become familiar with WWU values, the better equipped you are to get on with the business of enjoying the WWD while losing pounds and achieving your goal.

DESSERTS

Cakes			WWUS
(1/12th of 9" cake unless noted)	WWUS	Honey	3
		Honey spice	3
Almond	2	Marble, plain	3
Angel food, homemade	2	Marble, with boiled white icing	4
Apple, Duncan Hines	3		
Apple cobbler, frozen, Campbell's, 1 piece	2	Plain cake with boiled white icing	3
Banana	3	Plain cake with chocolate icing	4
Banana applesauce, plain	2	Plain cake without icing	3
Boston cream pie, Mrs. Smith's, 1/16th	4	Plain cake with uncooked white icing	4
Brownie with nuts, 2" × 2" × 3/4"	2	Pound cake, 3" × 3" × 1/2"	2
Caramel	3	Shortcake, 1 piece	2
Carrot	3	Shortcake with blackberries, 1 serving	4
Cheesecake, Jell-O, 1/8th	3		
Cheesecake, Sara Lee, 1/6th	3	Shortcake with peaches, 1 serving	3
Chocolate, plain, 3" × 3" × 2"	4	Shortcake with raspberries, 1 serving	4
Chocolate, with chocolate icing	6	Shortcake with strawberries, 1 serving	5
Chocolate, with vanilla icing	6		
Fruit, dark or light, 2" × 11/2" × 1/4", 1/2 ounce	2	Spice cake	3
		Sponge cake	3
Gingerbread, 3" × 3" × 2"	4	White or yellow cake plain	3

	WWUS		WWUS
White or yellow cake with caramel icing	4	Cinnamon crisp, 2 pieces	1
White or yellow cake with chocolate icing	4	Coconut bar	1
		Commodore	1
		Cream Lunch	1

COOKIES

(1 piece unless noted)

	WWUS		WWUS
		Dresden, Pepperidge Farm	2
Almond, Chinese	2	Fig bar	2
Almond Crescent, Nabisco	1	Fortune cookie	1
Animal Crackers, 5 pieces	1	Fruit, iced	2
		Fudge	1
Anisette, sponge or toast	1	Ginger snap, 2 pieces	1
Applesauce, iced	2	Hydrox, regular or mint	1
Applesauce, Sunshine	2	Ladyfingers	1
Arrowroot, 2 pieces	1	Lemon	2
Assortment	1	Lemon Coolers, 2 pieces	1
Bordeaux, Pepperidge Farm	1	Lemon Snaps, 3 pieces	1
Butter, 2 pieces	1	Lido, Pepperidge Farm	2
Butterscotch Fudgies, 1 ounce	2	Lisbon, Pepperidge Farm, 2 pieces	1
Cherry Coolers, 2 pieces	1	Macaroon	2
Chocolate	2	Mallo Puffs	1
Chocolate chip, commercial	1	Marshmallow, chocolate-coated	1
Chocolate chip, homemade	2	McDonaldland, 1 box	4
		Milano, Pepperidge Farm	1
Chocolate snaps, 2 pieces	1	Molasses	2
		Oatmeal	2
		Oreo	1

	WWUS		WWUS
Peanut Butter Cream Patties, 1/2 oz.	1	Ice Milk, vanilla, chocolate, strawberry	2
Pecan Sandies	2	Strawberry	3
Pfefferneuse	1	Vanilla	4
Pirouette	1	Vanilla, Häagen-Dazs	7
Pitter Patter	2	Vanilla, Howard Johnson's	5
Pizzelle	1	Vanilla, Schrafft's	4
Raisin Fruit Biscuit	1		
Sandwich Cremes	1	**ICE CREAM AND ICE SPECIALTIES**	
Shortbread, Lorna Doone	1		
Social Tea biscuit, 2 pieces	1	Chocolate-coated vanilla ice cream bar	2
Sugar, 1 ounce	2	Creamsicle	2
Sugar Wafer, 2 pieces	1	Drumstick	3
Vanilla Snap, 3 pieces	1	Fruit ice, 1/2 cup	2
Vanilla Wafer, 3 pieces	1	Fudgsicle	2
Vienna Fingers	1	Hot fudge sundae	4
Waffle Creme	1	Ice cream cone, cone only	1
		Popsicle, chocolate	2
ICE CREAM		Popsicle, fruit-flavored	1
(1 cup unless noted)		Sandwich, ice cream	2
		Sherbet, 1/2 cup	2
Chocolate	4	Spumoni	2
Chocolate, Häagen-Dazs	7	Strawberry sundae	4
Chocolate, Howard Johnson's	6	Tortoni	2
Chocolate, Schrafft's	5		
French frozen custard	3	**PIES**	
French vanilla	5	*(1/8th serving of 9" pie unless noted)*	
Ice Milk, soft-serve, vanilla, chocolate, strawberry	2	Apple, frozen, cooked, 1/6th	5
		Apple, homemade	4

	WWUS		WWUS
Apple, Hostess	5	Custard, homemade	4
Apple, McDonald's	4	Dutch Apple Bavarian cream, frozen, Sara Lee, 1/6th	3
Banana cream, frozen, Morton, 1/6th	3		
Banana custard, homemade	4	Lemon, Hostess, 1/6th	6
		Lemon chiffon, homemade	4
Blackberry, homemade	5		
Blueberry, frozen, Morton, 1/6th	3	Lemon meringue, homemade	4
Blueberry, homemade	5	Lime, Bavarian cream, Sara Lee, 1/6th	3
Butterscotch, homemade	6		
		Mince, frozen, Morton, 1/6th	4
Butterscotch cream	3		
Cherry, frozen, cooked, Mrs. Smith's, 1/6th	4	Mince, homemade	6
Cherry, homemade	5	Peach, homemade	4
Cherry, Hostess	6	Pecan, homemade	6
Cherry, McDonald's	4	Pie crust, baked, 9" shell, 1	12
Chocolate, Bavarian cream, frozen, Sara Lee, 1/6th	4		
		Pop Tart, all varieties, 1	3
Chocolate chiffon, homemade	3	Pumpkin, homemade	3
		Raisin, homemade	4
Chocolate chip Bavarian cream, frozen, Sara Lee, 1/6th	3	Rhubarb, homemade	5
		Shoofly, Pennsylvania Dutch, homemade	6
Chocolate meringue, homemade	4	Strawberry, homemade	3
Coconut cream, frozen, Morton, 1/6th	4	Strawberry cream, frozen, Morton, 1/6th	4
Coconut custard, homemade	4	Sweet potato, homemade	4

WWUS

PUDDINGS, MOUSSES, AND GELATINS

(1/2 cup unless noted)

	WWUS
Banana pudding	2
Bread pudding	3
Bread pudding with raisins	4
Butterscotch	2
Chocolate, Cool 'n Creamy, light and dark	3
Chocolate pudding, cornstarch base	3
Chocolate pudding, from mix	2
Custard, baked	4
D-Zerta, low-calorie with skim milk	2
Flan	4
Gelatin, fruit-flavored	2
Gelatin, fruit-flavored with fruit	2
Hunt's Snack Pack pudding	3
Indian, baked	2
Mousse, chocolate	7
Prune Whip	1
Pudding Mixer, rennet type, chocolate	2
Pudding Mixer, vanilla fruit	2
Rice pudding with raisins	3

WWUS

	WWUS
Tapioca chocolate	3
Tapioca cream	3
Vanilla	2
Zabaglione	2

OTHER

	WWUS
Apple Brown Betty, 1/2 cup	2
Buñuelos (fried pastries), 2	2
Chocolate cupcake, cream-filled, 1	3
Coffee cake, Drake's, 1	3
Cream puff with custard filling	4
Cream puff with whipped cream	4
Cupcake, filled, Hostess, 1	2
Danish pastry, fruit-filled, 41/2"	4
Danish pastry, plain, 41/2"	4
Devil dog, Drake's, 1	3
Ding Dong, Hostess, 1	2
Doughnut, cake-type, frosted, 35/8" × 11/2"	4
Doughnut, cake-type, plain, 35/8" × 11/2"	3
Doughnut, raised, creme-filled, 33/4"	3
Doughnut, raised, plain or powdered, 33/4"	3

	WWUS		WWUS
Eclair, custard-filled, chocolate icing, 5″ × 2″	3	Snowballs, Hostess, 1	2
		Sopapaillas (pastry puff), 2	2
Raisin snack cupcake junior, 1	2	Susie Q's, Hostess, 1	3
		Twinkies, Hostess, 1	2

DAIRY

CHEESE

(1 ounce unless noted)	WWUS		WWUS
The values expressed for hard and semi-soft cheeses are based on their high fat content.		Cream, whipped, 2 tablespoons	1
		Edam	2
		Feta	2
American	2	Farmer	1
Bleu or Roquefort	2	Gouda	2
Brick	2	Gruyère	2
Camembert	2	Jack	2
Caraway	2	Kisses, 1 piece	1
Chantelli	2	Liederkranz, Borden	2
Cheddar	2	Limburger	2
Cottage, creamed, plain, 1/4 cup	1	Monterey Jack	2
		Mozzarella	2
Cottage, creamed, with chives, 1/4 cup	1	Muenster	2
		Neufchatel	2
Cottage, creamed, with pineapple, 1/4 cup	1	Parmesan	2
		Parmesan, grated, 1 tablespoon	1
Cottage, low-fat, 1/4 cup	1	Port Salut	2
Cottage, uncreamed, plain, 1/4 cup	1	Provolone	2
		Ricotta	1
Cottage, uncreamed, pot-style, 1/4 cup	1	Romano	2
Cream	2	Swiss	2

WWUS

CREAM

	WWUS
Cream, Half & Half, 3 tablespoons	1
Cream, heavy, 1 tablespoon	1
Cream, light, 2 tablespoons	1
Cream, sour, 3 tablespoons	1
Cream, whipped, medium, 1 tablespoon	1
Cream, whipped topping, pressurized, 5 tablespoons	1
Cream, whipping, heavy, unwhipped, 1 tablespoon	1
Cream, whipping, light, unwhipped, 1 tablespoon	1

MILK

Buttermilk, 1 cup	1
Condensed, sweet, canned, 1 cup	13
Dry, nonfat, 1/3 cup	1
Dry, whole, 1/4 cup	3
Evaporated, canned, 1 cup	4
Low-fat, 1 cup	2
Nonfat (skim), 1 cup	1

	WWUS
Part skimmed, 2% milk solids added, 1 cup	2
Whole, 1/3 cup	1

MILK DRINKS
(1 cup)

Chocolate milk, 1% fat	2
Chocolate milk, 2% fat, whole	3
Chocolate milk with malt, whole	3
Chocolate milk with Ovaltine, skim	3
Chocolate milk with Ovaltine, whole	3
Cocoa mix	3
Eggnog	4
Instant Breakfast, vanilla, Carnation, whole milk	4
Malted milk	3
Milk shake, fast-food restaurant	4
Milk shake, homemade	5

MILK, OTHER
(1 cup)

Coconut	8
Coconut water	1
Goat	2
Soybean	2

	WWUS		WWUS
YOGURT		Raspberry and other	3
(1 cup unless noted)		fruit yogurt	
		Whole milk, plain	2
Frozen, 1/2 cup	1		
Part skim, plain	1		

BEVERAGES

ALCOHOLIC BEVERAGES			WWUS
Ale		Pabst	2
		Pabst Extra Light	1
(12-ounce serving)	WWUS	Rheingold	2
		Schlitz	2
Black Horse	2	Schlitz Lite	1
Black Horse, mild	2	Schmidt	2
Red Cap	2	Stroh's	2
		Tuborg	2

Beer

(12-ounce serving)

Distilled Liquor

(1 ounce, plain, on the rocks, with water, club soda, mineral water, or sugar-free mixers)

Black Label	2		
Budweiser	2		
Budweiser Lite	2		
Busch	2	Bourbon whiskey	
Coors	2	80 proof	1
Gablinger's	1	86 proof	1
Heidelburg	2	90 proof	2
Knickerbocker	2	100 proof	2
Meister Brau Light	1	Brandy, unflavored	
Meister Brau Premium	2	80 proof	1
Michelob	2	86 proof	1
Michelob Lite	1	90 proof	2
Miller	2	100 proof	2
Miller Lite	1	Canadian whiskey	
Narragansett	2	80 proof	1
Natural Light	1		

	WWUS		WWUS
86 proof	1	Vodka	
90 proof	2	80 proof	1
100 proof	2	86 proof	1
Gin		90 proof	2
80 proof	1	100 proof	2
86 proof	1		
90 proof	2	*Wine*	
100 proof	2	*(per 6-ounce glass)*	
Irish whiskey		Asti Spumante	3
80 proof	1	Catawba, pink	2
86 proof	1	Catawba, white	2
90 proof	2	Barbera	2
100 proof	2	Bardolino	2
Rum		Blackberry Wine,	4
80 proof	1	Mogen David	
86 proof	1	Bordeaux	2
90 proof	2	Burgundy, sparkling	2
100 proof	2	Burgundy, white and	2
Rye whiskey		red	
80 proof	1	Chablis, pink and	2
86 proof	1	white	
90 proof	2	Champagne, dry, pink,	2
100 proof	2	white, domestic,	
Southern Comfort		imported	
80 proof	1	Chateau Blanc	2
86 proof	1	Chateau Rouge	2
90 proof	2	Chateauneuf-du-Pape	2
100 proof	2	Chelors	2
Tequila		Cherry, Mogen David	3
80 proof	1	Chenin Blanc	2
86 proof	1	Chianti	2
90 proof	2	Claret	2
100 proof	2	Cognac	2

	WWUS		WWUS
Cold Duck	2	*Liqueurs*	
Dessert Petri	3	*(per 1 ounce serving)*	
Folle Blanche	3	Absinthe	2
Great Western, red, white	2	Amaretto	2
		Anisette	2
Madeira	3	Apricot	2
Muscatel	4	Banana	2
Port	4	B & B	2
Pouilly-Fuissé	2	Benedictine	2
Pouilly-Fumé	2	Bitters	2
Rhine	2	Blackberry	2
Riesling	2	Brandy	
Ripple, red and white	2	Apricot	2
Riunite, red and white	3	Blackberry	2
Rosé	2	Cherry	2
Sangria, pink and white	3	Coffee	2
		Ginger	2
Sauterne, Burgundy or cooking	3	Peach	2
		Cherry Heering	2
Sauterne, French white	2	Creme d'Amande	2
Sherry cocktail, Gold Seal	3	Creme d'Apricot	1
		Creme de Banane, Garnier	2
Sherry cocktail, Petri	3		
Sherry, cooking	3	Creme de Banane, Old Mr. Boston	1
Sherry, cream	4	Creme de Blackberry, Old Mr. Boston	1
Sherry, dry	2		
Sherry, Dry Sack	3	Creme de Cacao	2
Tokay	3	Creme de Café	2
Vermouth, dry and extra dry	3	Creme de Cassis	2
		Creme de Cherry	2
Vermouth, sweet and white	4	Creme de Coffee, Old Mr. Boston	1

	WWUS		WWUS
Creme de Menthe, Green, White	2	Gin and tonic	3
		Gin Rickey	2
Creme de Noyaux	2	Highball, with mixer	2
Creme de Peach	1	Hot buttered rum	3
Curaçao	2	Mai Tai	3
Drambuie	2	Manhattan, dry vermouth	2
Grand Marnier	2	
Grenadine syrup, alcoholic and nonalcoholic	2	Manhattan, sweet vermouth	2
		Margarita	2
Kahlúa	2	Margarita, banana or strawberry	3
Midori	2	
Peach	2	Martini, dry, extra dry, medium	2
Pernod	2	
Sloe Gin	2	Martini, sweet	2
Triple Sec	2	Mint julep	3
Vandermint	2	Old-Fashioned	2
		Piña colada	4
Mixed Drinks		Pink Lady	2
(as recommended in Official Bartender's Guide)		Planter's Punch	3
		Rob Roy	2
Bacardi cocktail	2	Rum sour	2
Black Russian	4	Screwdriver	3
Bloody Mary	2	Sloe gin fizz	3
Brandy Alexander	4	Sombrero	2
Brandy eggnog	5	Stinger	3
Champagne cocktail	3	Tequila Sunrise	3
Cuba libre	3	Tom Collins	2
Daiquiri	2	Vodka and tonic	3
Daiquiri, frozen	2	Vodka Collins	2
Daiquiri, frozen, banana or strawberry	3	Vodka sour	2
		Ward Eight	3
Gimlet cocktail	2	Whiskey sour	2

WWUS

COFFEE AND TEA

Coffee and tea, black, no sugar, or sweetened with artificial sweeteners, have a WWU of 0.

	WWUS
Coffee, 1 cup, black, 1–3 teaspoons sugar	1
Coffee, 1 cup, ½ ounce cream	1
Coffee, 1 cup, ½ ounce cream, 1–3 teaspoons sugar	1
Coffee, 1 cup, ½ ounce milk, 1–3 teaspoons sugar	1
Coffee, 1 cup, 1–2 teaspoons nondairy creamer	1
Coffee, 1 cup, 1–2 teaspoons nondairy creamer, 1–3 teaspoons sugar	1
Coffee, grain beverages, 1 cup, black	0
Coffee, grain beverages, Postum, 1 cup black	0
Coffee, International Flavors, General Foods, 1 cup	
Almond Mocha	2
Bavarian Mint	2
Cafe Français	1

	WWUS
Cafe Capri	1
Cafe Vienna	1
Cafe Viennese	1
Orange Cappuccino	1
Suisse Mocha	1
Tea, 1 cup, ½ ounce milk, 1–3 teaspoons sugar	1
Tea, 1 cup, with lemon	0
Tea mix, iced, 12 ounces, with or without lemon, no sugar	0
Tea mix, iced, 12 ounces, with or without lemon, pre-sweetened	2

SOFT DRINKS
(12 ounces unless noted)
All sugar-free diet sodas have a WWU of 0.

	WWUS
Bitter Lemon soda	3
Cactus Cooler soda	3
Chocolate soda	2
Coca-Cola	2
Cola, other brand names	2
Collins mixer	2
Cream soda	2
Dr Pepper	2
Fruit-flavored sodas	2
Funny-Face, all flavors	2

	WWUS		WWUS
Gatorade, citrus and cola	2	Apple juice, unsweetened, 1/2 cup	1
Ginger ale	2	Apricot juice, unsweetened, 1/2 cup	1
Grape soda	2		
Hawaiian Punch	3	Apricot nectar, 1/2 cup	1
Hawaiian Punch, low-calorie	2	Blackberry juice, unsweetened, 1/2 cup	1
Hi-C, all flavors	2	Blueberry juice, unsweetened, 1/2 cup	1
Lemonade	2		
Lemon-lime soda	2	Carrot juice, 1 cup	1
Limeade	2	Cranberry juice cocktail, sweetened, 1/2 cup	2
Mountain Dew	2		
Mr. Pibb	2		
Pepsi-Cola	2	Cranberry juice cocktail, unsweetened, 1/2 cup	1
Pepsi Light	2		
Purple Passion	2		
Quinine soda	2	Grapefruit juice, fresh, 1/2 cup	1
Root beer	2		
Seven-Up	2	Grapefruit juice, sweetened, 1/2 cup	2
Sprite	2		
Start	2	Grape juice, 1/2 cup	1
Tahitian Treat	3	Grape juice drink, 1/2 cup	2
Tang, all flavors	2		
Teem	2	Lemonade, 8 ounces	2
Tonic water	2	Lemon juice, 1/2 cup	1
Vanilla cream soda	3	Limeade, 8 ounces	2
Upper 10	2	Lime juice, 1/2 cup	1
Vernor's	2	Orange-apricot juice drink, 1/2 cup	2
Wink	3		
		Orange-grapefruit juice, sweetened, 1/2 cup	2
FRUIT JUICES			
Apple juice, sweetened, 1/2 cup	2	Orange juice, fresh, unsweetened, 1/2 cup	1

	WWUS		WWUS
Orange juice, sweetened, 1/2 cup	2	Prune juice, unsweetened, 1/3 cup	1
Orange juice drink, 1 cup	2	Raspberry juice, unsweetened, 1/2 cup	1
Peach nectar, 1/2 cup	1	Tangelo juice, unsweetened, 1/2 cup	1
Pear nectar, 1/2 cup	1		
Pineapple-grapefruit juice drink, 1/2 cup	1	Tangerine juice, unsweetened, 1/2 cup	2
Pineapple juice, 1/2 cup	1	Tomato juice, 1 cup	1
Pineapple-orange juice drink, 1/2 cup	1	Tomato juice cocktail, 1 cup	1
Prune juice, sweetened, 1/2 cup	2		

CHAPTER 10

Dieting Seven Days a Week:
The Flexi-Diet

Some diets work for some people some of the time; no diet works for all of the people all the time. We are not all alike. Our tastes and life-styles vary greatly. We diet differently and we lose weight differently. Is it any wonder, then, that in the weight-loss marketplace, there are so many diets to choose from?

Where Do Diets Come From?

From the paintings of the eighteenth and nineteenth centuries, you'll notice that the full figure—especially for women—was the style. A plump body was a sign of affluence and social distinction, therefore admired. Today it is neither healthy, admirable, nor fashionable to be overweight. To the contrary. There is nothing less true than that every-body loves a fat man or woman.

Although it is probable that obesity took the same toll of health and longevity then that it does today, in past centuries the connection between fat and physical ills was not made. Not until the twentieth century was obesity considered a disease or given wide medical atten-tion.

Before that time, however, in 1881 there was at least one man who experimented and cured a specific illness through weight loss. This man was Dr. William Harvey, an English ear surgeon. One of his patients,

William Banting, came to him with an earache. After careful examination of the corpulent, hard-of-hearing 60-year-old Banting, Dr. Harvey concluded that there was no disease and no sign of infection. He wondered if the excess fat was causing pressure on Banting's inner ear and thereby causing the earache.

Dr. Harvey put Banting on an unorthodox diet of venison, poultry, fish, and a limited amount of alcohol. No sugars or starches were permitted. One year later William Banting weighed in 46 pounds lighter and had perfect hearing. Flushed with success, William Banting published his own version of Dr. Harvey's diet and called it the Banting Diet. This diet was the first published weight-loss diet and was the forerunner of the high-protein, low-carbohydrate diets that followed in later years.

The next major diet phase focused on calorie counting. By 1930 doctors believed that excess food intake converted to excess fat. Even then it was recognized that some foods provided higher calories per serving than others. Obviously, sweets, cake, and candy were denser in calories than fruits, vegetables, and certain proteins. The reducing diets of the 1930s emphasized the importance of calories alone. The idea was to eat as few of them as possible. The calorie-counting theory ravished America, and calorie-counter books proliferated. No thought was given to the value of a particular food per se, nor to what it did or did not contribute to the body's total health. So people ate whatever foods they pleased as they counted their calories. Some people lost weight. Some people gained weight.

The course of diet history changed drastically in the late 1950s when Norman Joliffe, M.D., conceived the Prudent Men's Diet for members of an anticoronary club. Members of this group were middle-aged men, considered to be predisposed to coronary disease when they joined. The Prudent Diet Dr. Joliffe designed for them advocated neither excessive use of, nor complete abstention from, any one food. It did, however, limit intake of fatty meats, high-fat dairy products, eggs, hydrogenated shortenings, and foods containing any of these ingredients. After following the Prudent Diet for some time, their bodies slimmed down, their blood pressure decreased, and the expected rate of heart attacks was cut in half.

At this time Dr. Joliffe was the director of the Bureau of Nutrition of the Department of Health of the City of New York. From the feedback he received from the members of his anticoronary club he formulated a new type of reducing plan. His New York City Diet balanced proteins, carbohydrates, and fats within a calorie limit, 1,200 calories for women and 1,500 calories for men.

For the first time in history there was a recommended, easy-to-live-with diet on which people could lose weight. This successful plan was adopted by many weight-loss groups and clubs. And, finally, without suffering or starvation, many people were reaching their weight goals.

I was one of those people who experienced success by following a well-balanced eating plan that provided 1,200 calories per day. After having tried every fad diet that had come across the Brooklyn Bridge, in 1965, at 32 years of age, I finally shed my baby fat.

I've been asked many times as to the motivation behind my trying one more diet. And there are as many reasons as there are ingredients in any perfected recipe, but one incident does stand out in my mind as the push behind my new start. It happened at my weekly bridge game through the intervention of my friends. It was one of the most humiliating experiences of my life. I was asked to sit down and to listen. Then, as they all faced me, one of my friends said, "We're all worried about you. You're growing and growing. It looks as though each week before you come to the game, you stop at the gas station first and get yourself pumped full of air. We're afraid you're going to burst. Please, you've got to *do* something with yourself."

So I did something with myself. That week I went to a local diet group. I followed the son–of–New York City Diet, and it worked! I worked! I lost over one-third of myself—more than 40 pounds. I was thrilled. At last I was free of the fat in which I'd been encased for far too long, and finally I could get on with my life.

In the evangelical glow of my enthusiasm I believed that I could help everyone in the world to get thin. It was with that great goal and that energy and zeal that I dedicated myself to helping others lose weight by founding The Diet Workshop.

The Diet Workshop is unique in the weight-loss field because our mission is to teach healthy eating habits not only for weight loss but also forever. Losing weight is never an easy process, but we meet people halfway with our innovative programs and products. Further, it's our philosophy that once you've accomplished your weight loss, there is *nothing* in life you can't accomplish, within reason.

One of our innovative programs is the Flexi-Diet plan. The Flexi-Diet, child of the New York City Diet, was introduced in 1981. To help you keep all branches of the family tree straight, just think of the Wild Weekend Diet as the current version of the New York City Diet, with the Flexi-Diet as its immediate forebear, its parent.

All of the above diets share the common feature of providing 8,400 calories per week for women and 10,500 for men. All of them recommend a variety of food choices and a balanced eating plan featuring a protein and a carbohydrate at each meal.

The Flexi-Diet differs in presentation from its forerunners because it has two components: Core and Flexi. The Core Diet dictates the first 850 calories, and the dieter chooses the remaining calories to bring the daily total to 1,200 calories for women and 1,500 for men. The calories the dieter chooses are portioned into Flexi-Units. So, Flexi-Dieters add Flexi-Units each day. The Wild Weekend Diet brings its own variation to our diet table. As you know by now, the dieter follows a strictly controlled plan, the Weekday Slimdown Plan, during the week and then chooses any foods in the world to eat within his or her Wild Weekend budget on Saturday night and Sunday brunch.

Wild Weekend Units and Flexi-Units are the kissing cousins of the dieting world. Flexi-Units are what you use when you diet seven days a week *without* the Wild Weekend variation. More about the Flexi-Units later.

Following the Flexi-Diet offers a significant benefit. Because you handle food, controlling your choices daily, you actually learn how to maintain your weight loss from day one of dieting.

The Flexi-Diet is an alternative to the Wild Weekend Diet if you

like to have treats every day. Every day is a wild day! For those of you
who want to diet seven days a week and learn healthy eating habits for
a lifetime of thinness, Flexi is the way to go.

The Flexi-Diet offers you a world of food choices high in nutrition,
highly satisfying, yet calorie-controlled. The Core Diet gives choices
from seven categories: Protein, Grains, Lo Vegetables, Hi Vegetables,
Dairy, Fruit, and Flexi. All choices are broken into Units.

At breakfast on the Core Diet, you eat 1 Protein Unit and 1 Grain
Unit. For lunch you have 3 Protein Units, 1 Grain Unit, and Lo Vegetables. And dinner will be 4 Protein Units, 1 Hi Vegetable Unit, and
Lo Vegetables. Each day you also have 1 Dairy Unit, 2 Fruit Units, one
of which is citrus, and Flexi-Units. Look at the Core Diet displayed in
table form:

THE CORE DIET

BREAKFAST	LUNCH	DINNER
1 Protein Unit	3 Protein Units	4 Protein Units
1 Grain Unit	1 Grain Unit	1 Hi Vegetable Unit
	Lo Vegetables	Lo Vegetables

Daily: 1 Dairy Unit, 2 Fruit Units (1 citrus), and Flexi-Units.

Any time: Artificial sweetener, bouillon, coffee, diet beverages, 1 tablespoon diet dressing, diet gelatin, 2 teaspoons diet jelly, extracts,
herbs, lemon, lime, Lo Vegetables, mustard, pepper, salt, soy sauce,
spices, tea, vinegar, water, Worcestershire sauce.

The following are lists of the six food categories. An asterisk indicates the lowest-calorie foods in each category; a dagger indicates high
fiber.

Protein Units

(1 ounce cooked = 1 Unit, unless noted)

Cheeses
  *Cottage, ¼ cup

Farmer
Hard and feta

Limit, 4 ounces per
week
Ricotta
Chicken
  *Broiler
  Capon
  *Fryer
  Roaster
Cornish hen
Egg
    Limit, 4 per week
Finnan Haddie
*Fish, white-type
*Halibut
Liver
Salmon, canned or fresh
Sardines in mustard sauce
*Shellfish
  Clams
  Crab

Lobster
Mussels
Scallops
Shrimp
Swordfish
*Tofu
Tuna, drained
  oil-pack
  *water-pack
Turkey
  *Breast
  Dark meat
Veal
Limit to 3 meals weekly:
  Beef
  Frankfurters
  Ham
  Lamb
  Pork
  Tongue

GRAIN UNITS

Bagel, 1 ounce
Bread
  Plain, 1 ounce
  †Whole grain, 1 ounce
Bulgur, cooked, 1/4 cup
Cereal, cold, unsugared,
    2/3 ounce
†Cereal, cooked, 1/2 cup

Grits, cooked, 1/2 cup
Melba Rounds, 6
Muffin, English
  Plain, 1/2
  †Whole grain, 1/2
Pocket bread, 1 ounce
Roll, 1 ounce

Choose at least 1 whole grain serving per day.

Lo Vegetables

(Any time as desired)

†Asparagus
Bamboo shoots
Bok choy
Broccoli
†Brussels sprouts
†Cabbage
†Carrots
†Cauliflower
Celery
Cucumber
Daikon
Eggplant
†Leafy greens
Lettuce
†Mushrooms

†Onion, raw
†Peppers
Pickles, dill
Pimientos
Radishes
Rhubarb
Sauerkraut
Scallions
Spinach
Sprouts, all kinds
†Squash, summer
†String beans
†Tomato
Turnip
†Zucchini

Hi Vegetables

(1/2 cup = 1 Unit unless noted)

†*Artichoke
Beets
Corn, 1/2 ear or 1/2 cup
Mixed vegetables
Okra
†*Onion, cooked
Parsnip
†Peas
†Potato, small, baked or
    boiled

Pumpkin
Rutabaga
Squash, winter
Tomato puree
Tomato sauce
Vegetable juice, 12 ounces
Water chestnuts

Dairy Units

Buttermilk, 1 cup
Lowfat milk, 3/4 cup
Skim milk, 1 cup
Skim milk, evaporated,
   1/2 cup

Skim milk powder, 1/3 cup
Yogurt, lowfat, plain, 1 cup

Fruit Units

Apple, medium size
Apricot, 3 small
Banana, 1/2
*Berries, any kind, 1/2 cup
*Cantaloupe, 1/2 small
Cherries, fresh, 10
Figs, fresh, 1
*Fruit, water-packed, 1/2 cup
*Grapefruit, 1/2
Grapes, 1/2 cup
Honeydew, 2" wedge
Juice, unsweetened, 1/2 cup
Kiwi, 2
Mango, medium, 1/2
*Nectarine, medium size
Orange, medium size

Papaya, medium, 1/2
*Peach, medium size
Pear, medium size
*Pineapple
   canned in own juice,
     1/2 cup
   fresh, 1/2 cup
*Plums, 2 small
Prunes, 3
   juice, 1/3 cup
Tangelo, medium
Tangerine, medium size
Tomato, medium
   juice, 1 cup
Watermelon, 1 cup

All fruits except juices are good choices for high fiber.

Core Eating

On the Core Diet Plan you choose 1 Protein Unit and 1 Grain Unit for breakfast. Check out the Protein Unit category now. See that you might choose 1/4 cup of cottage cheese or 1 ounce of cooked shrimp or 1 egg or 1 ounce of hard cheese (Cheddar, Swiss, American, Gouda, etc.) or any of the other protein choices. Since you are allotted 1 Unit for breakfast, you choose *1.*

Now look at the Grain Unit category. Every item in the Grain Unit category is also 1 Unit, which is your breakfast allowance, so you may help yourself to 1 ounce of bagel (about a third of one) or half of an English muffin or 2/3 of an ounce of cold cereal or any of the other Grain Units. Please note: We recommend that one of your Grain Unit choices each day be whole grain.

Lunch and dinner per the Core Diet simply call for you to keep choosing the foods you like best. However, for lunch, you need to eat 3 Protein Units along with 1 Grain Unit and Lo Vegetables, and for dinner you choose 4 Protein Units, 1 Hi Vegetable Unit, and Lo Vegetables.

Each day on the Core Diet you will add 1 Dairy Unit at any time, 2 Fruit Units at any time, and Flexi-Units. Your Dairy Unit might be 8 ounces of skim milk or 3/4 cup lowfat milk or any of the other Dairy Units. Also choose two fruits from the Fruit Unit list, one of which must be citrus—1 orange or 1/2 grapefruit.

Flexi-Units

Flexi-Units are what make the Flexi-Diet fun and interesting. There are three types of Flexi-Units: CORE, MORE, and YOUR.

CORE Flexi-Units are:

1 Dairy Unit
1 Protein Unit
1 Hi Vegetable Unit
1 Grain Unit
1 Fruit Unit

MORE Flexi-Units are:

GRAINS
Barley, dry, 4 teaspoons
Bran, unprocessed, 1/4 cup
Cornmeal, cooked, 1/2 cup
Cornstarch, 2 tablespoons
Flour, 2 tablespoons
Macaroni, cooked, 1/2 cup
Matzo, 1/2 board
Noodles, cooked, 1/2 cup
Oysterettes, 20
Raisin bread, 1 ounce
Rice, brown, hot, cooked, 1/2 cup
Rice, white, hot, cooked, 1/2 cup
Rice, wild, cooked, 1/3 cup
Rice cakes, 2
Rusks, 5 (16 calories each)
Saltines, 4 squares
Spaghetti, cooked, 1/2 cup
Taco shells, 2
Tortilla, 6", 1
Wheat germ, 2 tablespoons

PROTEIN
Bologna, 3/4 ounce
Canadian bacon, 3/4 ounce
Herring, kippered or pickled, 1 ounce
Lox, 1 ounce

LEGUMES
Beans, baked, 1/4 cup
Beans, kidney, cooked, 1/3 cup
Beans, lima, cooked, 1/3 cup
Chick peas, 2 tablespoons
Lentils, cooked, 1/3 cup

DAIRY
Cream, half and half, 3 tablespoons
Cream cheese, whipped, 2 tablespoons
Ice milk, plain, 1/2 cup
Milk, whole, 1/3 cup
Yogurt, frozen, 1/2 cup
Yogurt, frozen, 1 stick

HI VEGETABLES
Avocado, small, 1/4
Potato, sweet, 1/2
Spaghetti sauce, plain, 1/3 cup

FRUIT
Cherries, maraschino, 6
Dates, pitted, 2
Figs, dried, 1
Fruit cocktail, juice packed, 1/2 cup
Persimmon, medium
Pomegranate, medium
Raisins, 1 ounce

FATS   LIMIT: 2 selections daily
Butter, 2 teaspoons
Butter, whipped, 1 tablespoon
Margarine, 2 teaspoons
Margarine, whipped, 1 tablespoon
Mayonnaise, 2 teaspoons
Oil, polyunsaturated
  Corn, 2 teaspoons
  Safflower, 2 teaspoons
  Sunflower, 2 teaspoons

NUTS
Almonds, whole in shell, 12
Coconut, fresh or dried, shredded, 1/4 cup
Coconut meat, 1" × 1" × 1/2"

Cashews, roasted, 4
Peanuts, roasted in shell, 1/2 ounce
Peanuts, Spanish type, 25
Macadamia, roasted, 3
Pistachio, in shell, 15

SEEDS
Sesame, 1/2 ounce
Sunflower, 1/2 ounce

DRINKS
Beer, 8 ounces
Beer, light, 12 ounces
Bourbon, 1 ounce
Champagne, 3 ounces
Gin, 1 ounce
Rum, 1 ounce
Rye whiskey, 1 ounce
Scotch whiskey, 1 ounce
Vodka, 1 ounce
Wine, dry, red or white, 3 ounces

EXTRAS
Catsup, 3 tablespoons
Cocoa, plain, 2 tablespoons
Cranberry sauce, 2 tablespoons
Creamer, nondairy, 2 tablespoons
Gum, regular or sugarless, 8 sticks
Peanut butter, 2 teaspoons
Popcorn, air-popped, 3 cups
Popcorn, plain, 2 cups
Seafood cocktail sauce, 1/4 cup
Soup, meatless, non-creamed, 3/4 cup
Sugar cone, 1
Whipped topping, nondairy, 1/4 cup

YOUR Flexi-Units are *your* choice of any one food Unit from the Wild Weekend Unit listings in Chapters 7, 8, and 9. More about this later.

Following the Flexi-Diet

For the first week you are on the Flexi-Diet, use the Core Diet only. This will get your dieting off to a wonderful start with a wonderful weight loss.

On week two, you add CORE Flexi-Units *only:* Women add 1 to 5 CORE Flexi-Units and Men 5 to 8 CORE Flexi-Units. Every day. Your choice. This means you can eat more of those foods that are on the Flexi-Diet food lists. You can eat these foods at meals or as snacks.

If you would like to have more chicken for lunch or dinner, you just use the CORE Flexi-Unit of Protein and eat another ounce of chicken. And if you're really hungry for chicken, you may use 2 CORE Flexi-Units of chicken, or even 3. All is up to you and your taste.

On week three and thereafter, you are permitted to choose foods from either the CORE Flexi-Units *or* the MORE Flexi-Units lists. So, eat the additional Flexi-Units in chicken again if you choose. Or, if you prefer, have a sugar cone of ice milk for 2 Flexi-Units (one MORE Flexi-Unit for ice milk and one for the sugar cone). Your allowance remains fixed: 1 to 5 Flexi-Units for Women (either CORE or MORE); men 5 to 8.

Now some words about YOUR Flexi-Units. At some point in your dieting process, or perhaps on maintenance, you may enlarge your Flexi-Unit list to encompass *all* the Wild Weekend Unit foods that have a unit value of 1. That is YOUR Flexi-Unit List.

What makes the Flexi-Diet fun is that you get to choose the foods you eat from a wide range of options each day. The Flexi-Diet is *your* diet.

At The Diet Workshop we believe that the diet you will stay on the longest and be the most successful with is the diet that you design yourself.

You'll continue to lose weight as long as you stay within the Core Diet and, restricting your *total* Flexi-Unit intake to 5 if you're a woman, 8 if you're a man. This holds true no matter from which Flexi-Unit list you choose your foods.

The following are some sample menus that will show you how to follow the Flexi-Diet correctly.

Sample Core Diet

Here's a sample Week One menu of the Core Diet with no Flexi-Units. It does contain "Add Daily" 2 Fruit Units and 1 Dairy Unit, all of which are marked with an asterisk.

CORE DIET	SAMPLE CORE MENU

Breakfast

1 Protein Unit	1 scrambled egg
1 Grain Unit	1/2 English muffin, toasted
	*1/2 cup grapefruit juice

Lunch

3 Protein Units	3 ounces tuna, water-pack
1 Grain Unit	1 ounce whole wheat bread
1 Lo Vegetable Unit	1 cup lettuce

Dinner

4 Protein Units	4 ounces broiled chicken
1 Lo Vegetable Unit	1 cup cauliflower
1 Hi Vegetable Unit	1/2 cup beets

Daily

| *2 Fruit Units (1 citrus) | Milk-shake: Blend together |
| | *1 cup skim milk |

*1 Dairy Unit   *1/2 cup frozen, un-
                                   sweetened strawberries
                                   artificial sweetener

The following is a sample Week Two menu of the Core Diet plus 3
CORE Flexi-Units. It also contains the daily 2 Fruit Units and 1 Dairy
Unit. The 3 Flexi-Units are marked with a +1. The "Add Daily" Fruit
and Milk Units are marked with an *.

CORE DIET	SAMPLE CORE MENU PLUS 3 FLEXI-UNITS

Breakfast

1 Protein Unit	1 scrambled egg
1 Grain Unit	1/2 English muffin, toasted
	*1/2 cup grapefruit juice

Lunch

3 Protein Units	4 ounces tuna, water-pack +1
1 Grain Unit	2 ounces whole wheat toast +1
1 Lo Vegetable Unit	1 cup lettuce
	*10 fresh cherries

Dinner

4 Protein Units	4 ounces broiled chicken
1 Lo Vegetable Unit	1 cup cauliflower
1 Hi Vegetable Unit	1/2 cup beets
	1/2 ear corn +1
	*3/4 cup lowfat milk

Add Daily

| *2 Fruit Units | Indicated above with * |
| *1 Dairy Unit | |

Women: 1–5 Flexi-Units
Men: 5–8 Flexi-Units

This is another example of Week Two. This time we have added 5 CORE Flexi-Units to the Core Diet. Count the pluses; then add to 5.

CORE DIET	SAMPLE CORE MENU PLUS 5 FLEXI-UNITS

Breakfast

CORE DIET	SAMPLE CORE MENU
1 Protein Unit	2 scrambled eggs +1
1 Grain Unit	½ English muffin, toasted
	*½ cup grapefruit juice

Lunch

3 Protein Units	3 ounces tuna, water-pack
1 Grain Unit	1 ounce whole wheat bread
1 Lo Vegetable Unit	1 cup lettuce
	1 tomato
	*1 cup milk

Dinner

4 Protein Units	4 ounces broiled chicken
1 Lo Vegetable Unit	1 cup cauliflower
1 High Vegetable Unit	½ cup beets
	⅓ cup plain spaghetti sauce +1
	½ cup cooked pasta +1
	1 roll +1
	3 ounces Chablis wine +1
	*1 nectarine

Add Daily

*2 Fruit Units   Indicated above with *
*1 Dairy Unit

Women: 1–5 Flexi-Units
Men: 5–8 Flexi-Units

Here is a sample of a Week Three plan as it contains CORE and MORE Flexi-Units for a total of 8. Note the 2 additional Flexi-Units of broiled chicken in the dinner plan.

CORE DIET	SAMPLE CORE MENU PLUS 8 FLEXI-UNITS

Breakfast

1 Protein Unit	1 scrambled egg
1 Grain Unit	1 ounce lean ham +1
	1 whole English muffin +1
	*1/2 cup grapefruit juice

Lunch

3 Protein Units	3 ounces tuna, water-pack
1 Grain Unit	1 ounce whole wheat bread
1 Lo Vegetable Unit	1 cup lettuce
	1 cup cucumbers and chopped celery
	*1 cup fresh fruit salad +1

Dinner

| 4 Protein Units | 6 ounces broiled chicken +2 |
| 1 Lo Vegetable Unit | 1 cup cauliflower |

1 Hi Vegetable Unit ½ cup beets
1 dinner roll, 1 ounce
+2

Snack

diet gelatin topped with
¼ cup nondairy
whipped topping +1
*1 cup skim milk
2 cups popcorn +1

Add Daily

*2 Fruit Units Indicated above with *
*1 Dairy Unit

Women: 1–5 Flexi-Units
Men: 5–8 Flexi-Units

Children and Teenagers

Children and teenagers have special needs, and the following required *additions* to the Core Diet are recommended for them each day.

CHILD 6–12

9 Flexi-Units to be chosen exactly as follows:
    3 Dairy Units
    1 Fruit Unit
    2 Grain Units
        plus
    3 Flexi-Units

TEEN BOY 12–16

12 Flexi-Units to be chosen exactly as follows:
    3 Dairy Units
    3 Fruit Units
    1 Grain Unit

2 Protein Units
    plus
3 Flexi-Units

TEEN GIRL 12–16

7 Flexi-Units to be chosen exactly as follows:
    2 Dairy Units
    2 Fruit Units
        plus
    3 Flexi-Units

And Finally, Some Questions and Answers

Question: Can I stay on the Core Diet with no Flexi-Units added and lose weight more quickly?

Answer: Yes, but *only* for one week before adding Flexi-Units. Minimal nutrition needs will be met by women eating no less than 1 Flexi-Unit, men no less than 5.

Question: Can I vary the number of Flexi-Units I eat each day?

Answer: Sure, follow the Flexi-Diet any way you want; it's yours to design as you wish. Some people add fewer than their allowed Flexi-Units each day, Monday through Friday, and then eat their full daily allotment on Saturday and Sunday.

Question: I hate breakfast. Can I skip it and combine it with lunch?

Answer: Breakfast is an important meal. It gets you going for the day. We recommend eating three meals per day for optimal weight loss.

Question: I love a big breakfast. Can I combine it with lunch?

Answer: You can do better than that. We don't recommend combining a meal because that means you are skipping a meal, but you can use your Flexi-Units to eat as much protein, bread, and fruit as you'd like for breakfast and then eat lunch.

Question: I hate chicken, and you have it listed every night for dinner on the sample menu plans.

Answer: These are *sample* menu plans only, to show you how the program works. Choose any from the Protein Unit list that you like as a substitute.

Question: Can I mix my proteins and eat 2 Units of ham and 1 Unit of hard cheese for lunch?

Answer: Yes. You may mix and match your lunch Protein Units as you wish, providing you don't exceed the recommended number of Units.

CHAPTER 11

The Last Ten Pounds Plus Best Diet Tips

And Ten to Go . . .

The last ten pounds are the hardest. At this point you've probably been on the diet for a while, and your motivation and morale may be at a low ebb.

It's true, too, that you are dealing here with fat that's been stuck on your body the longest, so it's the toughest to get off. After all, that fat has been compacted over time by more fat accumulation. No wonder it's stubborn and resistant.

We are going to deal with this old fat in a special and effective way. We're going to put your diet on a diet. And here's how.

When you see the scale strike ten—pounds to go, that is—cut your Wild Weekend Units in half. If you are a woman, permit yourself only 18 WWUs for the weekend, and if you are a man, allow yourself only 23.

So, what that means is that on Saturday night women will eat 12 WWUs, men will eat 16 WWUs. For Sunday brunch women eat 6 WWUs, men 7.

This kind of dieting will boost your morale and your weight loss!

Best Diet Tips

By now you know a lot about the Wild Weekend Diet. But we're not done yet. We will give you even more tools to succeed; we will give you our best diet tips. Following are more than 100 helpful suggestions garnered from the world's most successful dieters and maintainers. You'll find these tips grouped into six major categories: Exercise; Awareness; Behavior Modification; Health; Stress Reduction; and Miscellaneous.

The lists that follow are a resource for you. I don't expect you'll follow every last suggestion, nor do I expect you to try a whole bunch at one time.

What I *do* expect is that you'll read them all. Then you will know that these aids are there for the time when you need the strength to diet one more day, because there will be those days. You will find them useful, also, when you are ready to become a Professional Eater.

A Professional Eater is a person who eats when and what s/he wants to and who keeps within goal range. Like any advanced activity, it takes time, effort, and experience to become a professional.

Exercise Tips

Many believe they cannot control the rate by which their bodies burn off fat. They think they're genetically predisposed, born, to burn fat at a set rate. Don't believe it—it's just not true. Simply stated, the more you move, the more you lose. Some experts believe that the benefits of exercising are long-lasting. They say that if you exercise briskly your body's metabolism will speed up and you'll continue burning calories at a faster rate for many hours after you've exercised.

If you exercise, you will tone up your muscles, get rid of excess flab, feel better in mind and body, sleep better, increase your stamina, handle stress more effectively, and like yourself better.

Any exercise is better than none at all. Start with realistic goals, like walking to your lunch date instead of riding, and build from there.

1. The best exercise is regular exercise. Don't force yourself to do conditioning exercises if you don't like them. Look instead for an activity you consider fun—swimming, tennis, golf, bicycling, long-distance walking, etc.

2. Choose an exercise that offers an aerobic workout, muscle strengthening, and muscle flexing. Aerobic exercise is exercise that raises your heart rate and consumes oxygen. Some aerobic exercises are: walking briskly at 3 miles an hour, jogging, jumping rope; all of these to be done for 30 minutes without a break. This is recommended three times a week for top physical condition.

3. Always warm up before strenuous exercise. Stretch all your muscles and run or walk briskly in place until your heart rate increases. This will help you avoid any injury to "cold," unstretched muscles.

4. Follow your workout with a "cool down." Do the same movements as in your warm-up. This will help you avoid the painful muscle tightening called cramps.

5. Start exercising gradually. Don't be one of those "weekend athletes," starting out like gangbusters on a Saturday morning and continuing through with 10-mile bike rides on Sunday. After not having been on a bicycle for 10 years, all that's going to happen with *that* strategy is that by Monday you'll be a bundle of aches and pains, with no further interest in physical fitness. So be smart. Start with walking. Walk briskly for 20 minutes three times a week. You can gradually increase the length of your walk, and then increase the frequency.

6. Don't overdo or underdo. It's quite natural to feel stretches and dull aches. However, if something hurts or gives you a sharp pain, stop.

7. Exercise at a pace at which you can carry on a normal conversation and not be short of breath.

8. Wear supportive, comfortable, and well-fitting shoes. The greatest deterrent to successful exercise is sore feet. After exercising, baby your darlings with a warm soak, cream or lotion, and a nice

cool powdering all over. Then elevate them on a pillow and feel virtuous.

9. Don't exercise on an empty stomach. You don't ask your car to run without gas. About 1–2 hours before your workout, have a light but nutritious meal. On the other hand, don't exercise on a full stomach. Allow time between your meal and exercise.

10. Exercising outdoors is truly invigorating. Try walking, golfing, tennis, swimming, bicycling, skiing, jogging, canoeing, paddleball, running, mountain climbing.

11. Winter's no excuse for hibernation. Get an exercise bicycle or an adaptor that will make your bike stationary for exercise in the house. Now you can fantasize cycling anywhere in the world (without the typhoons and hurricanes) while warm and comfortable in your own home. More indoor exercises: mini-trampolines; Ping-Pong; roller skating; ice skating; swimming; indoor tennis; racquetball; dancing; or squash.

12. You don't need a partner to exercise. There's something to be said for a long walk by yourself. Take this time to reflect, to get acquainted with yourself—and to review your diet, making plans for the slim new you!

13. Get into the whole exercise thing—buy yourself a new exercise suit.

14. Think about buying a portable music cassette player. Exercise is even better with music. Or take this time to play your foreign language tape. You might as well be slimming down while conjugating all those irregular verbs.

15. Don't get bored. Boredom is deadly. Vary your routine. Walk a different route, take a different companion, change your destination.

16. Wear a pedometer when you're walking to measure how far you've walked. See if you can beat your own record. Always look for chances to burn extra calories.

17. Carry the groceries to your car and then to your house.

18. Many people (who will remain nameless) accumulate piles at the bottom of the staircase. This is the I'll-take-them-all-up-later

syndrome. Now, in the name of calorie burning, here is your big chance to reform. Take whatever it is up as soon as you can. This trip will be good for your soul—and your hips.

19. Go out for the mail yourself.
20. Take the dog for a walk instead of putting him out.
21. Ignore the elevator or escalator; take the stairs. If you work on a high-numbered floor, walk to the second or third floor and catch the elevator there.
22. Always walk *down* the stairs.
23. Park your car as far away as possible from your destination. Carry an umbrella in case of rain.
24. Use the following to learn how many calories you burn by doing your favorite exercise. You will be proud each time you finish your exercise and won't want to ruin its effects by eating. Remember, *any exercise* is better than no exercise.

Activity	Weight*	Calories Burned
Walking briskly	120 pounds	308 per hour
Walking moderately	120 pounds	163 per hour
Walking briskly	150 pounds	401 per hour
Walking moderately	150 pounds	213 per hour
Running	120 pounds	500 per hour
Running	150 pounds	651 per hour
Bicycling	120 pounds	233 per hour
Bicycling	150 pounds	304 per hour
Swimming	120 pounds	180 per hour
Swimming	150 pounds	235 per hour
Jumping rope	120 pounds	388 per hour
Jumping rope	150 pounds	420 per hour

* Body weight influences number of calories burned. The heavier the body weight, the more energy expended in exercising.

MORE CALORIE/ACTIVITY INFORMATION:

Less than 1 calorie/minute

Sleeping, lying down

1–2 calories/minute

Sitting: reading, handwork,
    crafts, card playing, listening
    to music, eating, talking,
    typing, using business
    machines

2–3 calories/minute

Standing up: telephoning,
    making salad, stand-up crafts
Self-care: washing face,
    showering, shaving, setting
    hair
Light housekeeping: sweeping,
    dusting, picking up
Simple calisthenics and casual
    exercise, badminton

3–5 calories/minute

Brisk walking
Shopping

Washing car
Heavy housework: scrubbing
    floor, washing windows,
    making beds, vacuuming,
    ironing
Sports: bowling, dancing,
    exercising

More than 5 calories/minute

Walking up and down stairs
Mowing with handmower
Snow shoveling
Outdoor gardening
Jogging and running
Very active calisthenics: fast
    push-ups, jump rope
Tennis match
High-speed bicycling
Skiing
Active dancing
Steady swimming
Brisk game of golf (on foot)

Awareness

One of the keys to successful weight loss is to be aware of the pitfalls
you'll encounter in losing weight. Each of us has his or her own stum-
bling block. The following tips will help you follow through, on the
WSP, that straight and narrow road between Wild Weekends.

1. Food is lovely, as we all agree. But if it's always been your reward, find another. A scarf, a book, a ticket to the ball game—anything you can't eat.
2. Start a hobby—preferably something that keeps your hands busy and your mind off the refrigerator.
3. Don't test your willpower. If it were great you wouldn't be dieting.
4. Resist the urge to weigh yourself frequently. On the Wild Weekend Diet weigh yourself only once a week on a regular schedule. When you reach your goal, you can weigh yourself more often.
5. Get involved with activities that keep your morale high. It's easier to diet when you feel good about yourself.
6. During the week, keep no junk food in the house! The Wild Weekend is coming. Indulge yourself *then*, and not before.
7. If you want to snack between meals, take fruit, diet soda, or a small green salad.
8. If you live alone, you've got an advantage. There is *no reason* to have problem foods in the house. On the other hand, you may be tempted to skip regular meals altogether and snack all day. Don't. The nutritional cost is too high.
9. Don't feel obliged to hide the fact that you're dieting. You have the right to try to be your best and healthiest self. Remember, when worrying about the opinion of others, they do not live in your body. You do.
10. Eat three meals daily. Skipping breakfast and lunch only sets you up for an apocalypse at the dinner table and beyond.
11. Forget guilt. One goof does not a disaster make. You're not the first person to fall off the wagon. Just get back on it, like all the rest of us who are now slim.
12. Remember with the next mouthful that you are back on the Wild Weekend Diet.
13. Keep a diet diary. It's positively amazing how much food we all eat and then completely forget. Write down *everything* you eat every day for at least three weeks. Even broken cookies count!

14. Keep track of all the foods you resisted during the week. It will soon be evident to you how many calories you used to eat. Then brag to yourself about how strong and controlled you are about food.

15. Use awareness techniques. When your mind whispers "food" to you, lift up your hand and turn off that switch.

16. At the same time click your mind on to foodless pictures—an exotic foreign scene, a bubble bath, a new book, a phone call. Act on your mental picture.

17. Write yourself a letter and say good-bye to your fat. List every reason to hate the fat on your body, why it keeps you from doing what you want to do, keeps you from being who you want to be. Mail the letter and read it every time you want to overeat.

18. Find a picture of yourself when you were thin. You've never been thin? Okay, then cut out a picture of someone who now looks as you want to look. Then paste your face on that person's body. Put this picture where you can see it frequently during the day and during the evening, or put it next to your alarm clock so that it is the first thing you see every morning and the last thing you see every night. Say to yourself, "That's me!"

19. As you lose pounds and inches your clothes become too big for you. Tailor them down to your new size or get rid of them. If you know you have only clothes that fit, you'll have one more reason to stay thin.

20. If you are not working and don't wish to, find a volunteer organization that will expand your horizons. Expend some concern on others, not your stomach.

21. Don't be disappointed when others do not praise you for your weight loss. Some people are openly hostile to good losers because they cannot stand success of any kind in others. Remember always that you are conquering yourself. You can do anything!

22. Identify your weakness. If you eat because you are bored, start a new hobby. If you eat because you are lonely, join a club or dig out your library card and read, read, read. If you eat because you

are happy, tell yourself how much happier you'd be if you were thinner. If it's anger or depression that brings the hand to mouth, work out these emotions in a better way. Exercise, talk with a friend, see a counselor, or take a walk to a quiet, scenic place. Or scrub the floor or fix the step on the back porch. Do anything else, but don't eat your anger and depression. It will only eat you.

23. Study calories. If you learn that your favorite binge is 100 calories plus, some of the lure of that food will vanish.

Behavior Modification

Behavior modification, as it relates to weight loss, is the science of changing fat and negative thoughts and actions to thin and positive thoughts and actions. Most of us have spent a lifetime learning to be fat. The following tips will help you learn to be thin.

1. Practice eating as a solitary act. Eat your meals without watching television or reading the newspaper or a magazine. Concentrate on your food and savor every bite. Often when you are distracted while eating you don't experience the enjoyment of your food and you may go looking for more.

2. Eat sitting down. And only in a proper place, such as the kitchen or dining room table, at the picnic table or on a blanket or in a restaurant or in a lunchroom. When you stop giving yourself permission to eat standing up, you have removed a frequent cause of miseating.

3. Stop eating when your body tells you it is satisfied. Push your plate away and throw out the leftovers. If picking at the leftover food on your plate is a problem, and you can't immediately throw it away, sprinkle pepper or salt or sugar all over it.

4. Have only low-calorie beverages between meals. Practice the art of eating only during mealtimes.

5. Keep a journal of your feelings about dieting. Write down any frustrations you may have, and get rid of them by writing in-

stead of eating. Also, record how great you feel while dieting. This will help you stick with your positive eating plan.

6. Use smaller plates to serve your food. Servings will look larger . then. Deceive your eyes; you cannot con the scale.

7. Eat one mouthful of food at a time. Chew each bite thoroughly and swallow it before taking the next bite. This helps you eat more slowly and thereby fill up faster.

8. You do have control over food. Prove it by leaving some on the plate. Say no and mean it.

9. Eat slowly and consciously. Try eating with chopsticks or baby utensils or your opposite hand. These activities help you concentrate on eating and make the act of eating less automatic.

10. Put a standing mirror on your table and watch yourself eat. Many people are totally unaware of their rapid eating habits until they see themselves shoveling in the food. Pretend you are dining with a movie star, and as you eat, act chic, poised, and unhurried.

11. Stop and mentally okay food before eating. This is probably the most important of all behavior changes. When you learn *not* to eat what you do not need, you've won a victory over your fat.

12. Keep a record of people or situations that trigger the wrong eating habits. Make a list of the "binge" foods. You can control it by staying away from it. Same goes for people. You can still enjoy these people's company but not for lunch or dinner.

13. Eat only what you've planned in advance. Make out a week's menu and stick to it. Make no change or substitutions. Fill out your menu after you have eaten and then make a shopping list from your menu.

14. Shop by list only. Make up a weekly shopping list at home. Go through your cabinets and refrigerator to see what you need. When you get to the supermarket, buy only the foods on your list and take only enough cash with you for them. If this fails, send someone else to the store for you and tell them to buy *only* what you've listed.

15. Put your fork down between bites. Repeat the procedure to eat

only one mouthful at a time, then add to it by putting down your fork before taking the next bite. Take at least twenty minutes to eat your meals.

16. Enlist the support of your family and friends. Tell them you are dieting, and ask them to please give you a break and refrain from urging you to eat what you shouldn't.

17. Tell yourself that you will diet 100 percent this week. Promise yourself a perfect five days on the WSP. Each time you feel tempted to go off, tell yourself the Wild Weekend is coming.

18. Make out a personal reward list. Write down any and all gifts, pleasures, and activities you like. Then plan to select one reward at least three or four times per week. Being rewarded for making a change in behavior makes changing easier and more exciting.

19. Cook a new recipe each week. Try all of the WSP recipes in Chapter 4 at least once, and create your own, following the WSP cooking guidelines.

20. Exercise daily. Refer to the tips on exercise earlier in this chapter and get moving! While you are exercising you cannot eat.

21. Tell yourself three good things about yourself and your life each day. Build up your confidence and begin to appreciate how special and wonderful you really are. Tell yourself this over and over again until you believe it. You *should* believe it; it's true.

Health

Good health is precious—a birthright. But good health doesn't just fall your way; you can help yourself to better health by following these tips.

1. Sleep. Most of us require seven to eight hours of sleep per night to give the body the rest it needs to repair itself from the stress of the day. Be sure you get just the right amount of sleep your body requires. Too much or too little is not healthy.

2. Rest. This is different from sleep. Rest is the act of shutting everything down, if only for a few moments. "Stop the world

and get off" briefly, several times a day. Stare out the window and daydream for five or ten minutes. Close your office or bedroom door, prop up your feet, put your head back, and take several deep breaths before resuming your schedule. Take a fifteen-minute catnap—put your head down on the desk or table and let your weary mind wander. Set a clock if you tend to fall into a deep sleep.

3. Relax. Again, this is different from sleep and rest. You can relax in any situation. Even if you are in the middle of a board meeting or stuck in traffic, breathe deeply and regularly and tighten all your muscle groups, one group at a time, then relax them. You will feel refreshed and ready to go back to your activity.

4. Exercise. We've talked a lot in this chapter about the role of exercise in weight control. Exercise is vital to good health, and there's not a lot more to say about it except do it!

5. Take vitamins and mineral supplements, regardless of how little or how much you eat. Today's food supply does not contain the nutrients that were present in the foods your parents or grandparents ate. The soil is depleted. The environment wreaks havoc with nutrients. Modern food-processing techniques rob food of its nutrients, then food storage, transportation, and cooking deplete nutrients further. Good health is more assured by supplementing your everyday diet with vitamins and minerals.

6. Pleasure. Remember "All work and no play makes Jack a dull boy"? It's true. And our life in the fast lane often leaves little room for fun and pleasure. Make room. You owe it to your body and soul.

7. Eat good food. On the Wild Weekend Diet you have the foods of the world from which to choose. Make each choice a healthy choice. Make sure you're getting good nutrition in return for all the calories you are spending.

8. Reduce salt, sugar, and fat. The less of these you take in, the thinner and healthier you will be.

9. Check your blood pressure regularly. This is one illness that definitely can be controlled. If you don't have high blood pres-

sure, practicing good health measures will probably help you avoid it altogether.

10. Drink plenty of water. Water helps you feel less hungry, and it also washes out the body's impurities. Drink six to eight cups of pure water daily. Bottled water and spring water are good alternatives to the tea, coffee, or diet drinks.

11. Reduce your intake of alcohol and stop smoking. Take medications only as prescribed by your physician. Weight loss, good health, plenty of rest, relaxation, and exercise will surely lessen your frequency of trips to the doctor and your need for medications.

Stress Reduction

Stress is being pulled in more than one direction at once. It is positive as well as negative. Positive stress gives you an incentive to achieve good things. Stress is negative only when it is excessive. Too much stress is hazardous to your diet, your health, and your life.

The time clock, the executive meeting, the rude customer, the screaming boss, bumper-to-bumper traffic, the tailgaters, the stuck horn, the doctor's office, the dentist's drill, demanding children, getting fired, marriage, divorce, graduation, birth of a new baby, loss of a loved one—these events in our lives, pleasant and unpleasant, cause stress. Routine is stress. You cannot escape stress, but you can learn to live with it.

To reduce the harmful effects of stress in your life, follow these tips.

1. Avoid friction. Keep away from people and situations that cause you discomfort. You do not need unnecessary worry, concern, frustration, or grief.

2. Deal with difficulties head-on. In other words, stop procrastinating. Some people spend money or wasted hours agonizing about doing something they don't want to do or have a hard time doing. The problem, therefore, is always present, causing unnec-

essary stress. Do the hard things first in your day, and then the rest of the day will be "easier."

3. Exercise. Here it is again! Exercise reduces stress immensely. Clear your mind as you move all your muscles. Exercise rids your body of excess adrenaline caused by stress. Afterward you'll be relaxed, with an inner calmness and a better ability to deal with day-to-day problems. Exercise helps you function mentally much more efficiently. The best way to relax the mind is to move the legs.

4. Create a relaxing environment. Dim the lights and shut out noise. Close your eyes and practice deep, normal breathing. Slowly go through, one at a time, all the muscle groups in your body, tighten them, hold them, then relax them. Start with your feet, then your calves, then thighs, then buttocks, then abdomen, then chest and shoulder area, then upper arms, lower arms, hands, neck, and finally the face muscles. Then go back to see if you still feel any tense areas in your body. If you do, tighten those muscles again and relax them. Repeat this until all the tension in your body is gone. You will feel very relaxed and the physical stress will be gone.

5. Follow the Wild Weekend Diet or the Flexi-Diet plans. Being well nourished helps you to handle stress best.

6. Listen to soothing music. Sit down and put on an easy-listening record or tape.

7. Get a massage or learn to give yourself one. It is one of the best relaxers.

8. Change What You Can—Accept What You Cannot—Have the Wisdom to Know the Difference.

Miscellaneous

And, finally, here are a few more tips to help you realize your goal of being thinner!

1. Give yourself time to lose weight. You didn't get fat overnight and you won't get back to where you want to be overnight! A healthy average weight loss for women is 1–2 pounds per week after the first week. If a 1–2 pound loss is discouraging, imagine 1–2 pounds of hamburger sticking over each of your hips. And ask yourself, "Do I want that back?"

2. When you think you're beaten, you aren't. So, don't quit! Quitting is easy. Getting on with it isn't. But remember, at any point in your diet you *are* further ahead than when you began. Keep on going. Remember, "Quitters Never Win and Winners Never Quit!"

3. Life is a battle. So is dieting. Arm yourself for battles. If you know the party you are going to may offer too many temptations, be ready for it. Start telling yourself five days before that you will not overeat. Write this thought down. Believe it. Picture yourself at that party and not overeating. Rehearse this scene over and over again. When you do go to the party, your not-overeating behavior will be natural.

4. Jazz yourself up. You're eating good food, shedding fat, and changing on the inside. Do something for your outside. Try a new chic hairstyle, get a manicure, have a professional makeover (you can get one free at many department stores), color your hair, or buy dazzling, outrageous clothing accessories like colorful rope belts, teakwood and colored bead necklaces, a diamond stickpin or tie clasp. Decorate yourself, not a cake.

5. Take your measurements daily. Often weight loss is shown faster this way, and you will be rewarded quickly. A quarter of an inch off the waist is a great loss.

6. Make another list. Call it "How to Stay Fat." Write down every example you can think of, such as: picking at food while I cook; buying fattening goodies (in case company drops in); and, I ride when I can walk, etc. Then eliminate each of these habits one by one. You'll be on your way to eliminating fat at the same time.

7. Make contracts with family and friends. Ask your family to per-

form tasks in the kitchen that might cause you to miseat. In exchange you can offer to drive them to the movies on the weekend. Ask friends and co-workers to keep the sweets out of your environment, and in turn you will do_____for them. This works.

8. Change what you feed others. If you believe it's important to your health to avoid foods with empty (non-nutritious) calories, then it's important to the health of those you care about, too. Change your way of thinking when planning meals. The side benefit to you, of course, is that the food won't be around to tempt you.

9. When it comes to holiday planning, place your emphasis on the true meaning of the holiday at hand. Then plan activities to support this. Make the meal planning secondary. Consider food at the time to be necessary to well-being but not the reason for the celebration.

10. Become a proponent of "coffee and conversation." One successful dieter we know told the story of being invited to a neighbor's house for coffee. She was served her coffee and kept waiting for the "and." It never came. She left that neighbor's house insulted that day. Guess: Was the neighbor fat or thin? She was *thin!* Today our dieter is also thin, and when she invites someone for coffee, that's *all* she serves.

11. Eliminate such diet-breaking excuses from your vocabulary as "The devil made me do it," "I carry my weight well," "Broken cookies don't count," "My husband likes women who look like women." Instead, add to your vocabulary: "There is no reason why I shouldn't be thinner and healthier."

12. Surround yourself with your best friends: a full-length mirror, a scale and tape measure, cucumbers, celery and green and red pepper sticks, the Wild Weekend Diet, and a cobra in your refrigerator!

13. Practice the dieter's exercises of placing both of your hands on the edge of the table and pushing away. Shake your head from

left to right, often. Reach for your mate instead of your plate. Run past the doughnut shop.

14. Remember the dieting rewards: flowers, escape weekends, health-club memberships, facials, massages, stereo radios with headphones.

15. Fat-proof your environment. Get the cookies out of the clothes hamper. Remove the jelly beans from the lingerie drawer. Take the candy bars out of your desk and the chips out of your glove compartment. Put marbles in the candy dish (or colored soaps or pretty seashells). Put a piranha in the cookie jar.

16. Take your diet one day at a time. Learn all that you can about yourself and make small changes one at a time. This way you won't feel discouraged, and you will go further in your success than you ever imagined!

17. When you eat or drink *naked* foods (not mixed with Hot List items or prepared according to the Hot List methods), your dieting will go best.

18. Paper your house, your desk, your car, and the cat with motivators. Make a copy of each of the following statements and put them where you will see them every day, many times a day.

- Temptations only come in the door you leave open.
- The best meal lasts but a few hours. Thin lasts forever.
- Feeling good is wearing your shirt tucked in.
- Don't watch your weight, lose it!
- What you eat in private shows up in public.
- If you learned to be fat, you can learn to be thin.
- Think thin! Act thin! Be thin!

CHAPTER 12

The Chinese Curse, Maintenance, and a New Beginning

The Chinese Curse

Have you heard of the Chinese curse? It says, "May you live in interesting times."

One of the most interesting circumstances of life is change. In achieving a weight-loss goal you've made a change, a change in your appearance, and perhaps a change because you allowed yourself to be successful. For many people significant weight loss is the first real success in their lives. Perhaps this is true for you.

Whether this is your first success, or one of many, you face a new question: Now what?

You pulled it off, you saw it through; you lost weight, and it wasn't easy—it never is—but you did it. What do you do for an encore? You can't ride on the crest of that dieting success forever. The Chinese curse applies to us all; we *all* need new goals to work for. In your case the goal is maintenance—staying slim forever.

A New Beginning

There is a story told about the founder of judo. As you may know, judo, like all martial arts, marks success and progression by the color of belts. The beginners are given a white belt, and through a series of steps and achievements, they may work their way up to a black belt.

The black belt proclaims to you and to the world that you are a master with the skill, the dedication, the discipline, and the perseverance to achieve on the highest level.

One day, as the founder of judo lay very old and ill in bed, a disciple came to him and asked that he share the secrets of his expertise with his followers. The founder agreed to do this and expressed his secret in a single thought: Each time you attempt a new step, seek a new level, choose a new goal requiring new techniques, a new discipline, *you must put on your white belt* anew and begin again at the beginning.

Each of you has, to a greater or lesser degree, struggled to achieve your goal-range weight. You will find that maintaining this weight loss is a new challenge and requires a new struggle.

Consider yourself an expert at dieting and a novice at maintenance. Award yourself the black belt for having achieved success, and then put your white belt on and learn how to maintain that weight loss.

You have a new goal but the same needs. Recognize that you must begin again. Your objective is different, but the vigilance and discipline needed are the same. As before, you need information, techniques, and motivation to maintain your weight loss.

The Second Decision

Losing weight required a decision on your part. You made that decision and you lost weight. Now you must make a second decision—to be thin forever. And just as you took the time and the effort to learn about a diet and behaviors that ensured your personal weight loss, so, too, must you come up with a personal maintenance package that is right for you. For most of us, maintaining is more challenging and frustrating than dieting. Dieting is difficult, but it is also very simple. When you subtract calories from your intake, you subtract pounds from your body, and eventually the job is done; you're within goal range. By the time you've gotten down to where you want to be you have a good idea what you have to do to burn up the fat. Maintenance is not so simple; on maintenance you must write your own script.

Keeping It Off

If you had any hope of going back to your old style of eating now that you are at your goal, abandon that hope. Listen to your inner voice of reason as it tells you that if you go back to your old style of eating you'll go back to your old, fat figure as well.

As during the weight-loss process, on maintenance, ignorance is not bliss. It is disaster. Some things you must know.

Calories

You must know how many calories you burn up each day. Many women do not believe that 3,500 calories equal a pound. Some women believe that they gain weight by simply *smelling* the wrappers that contain food. Not a fact. Smelling does not put on pounds. Neither does looking. Eating does. So what holds true for most women is that they burn from 11 to 12 calories per pound of their ideal weight each day. For men this number varies between 14 through 17. Men are, in general, larger than women, weigh more, and consequently, they get to eat more without the penalty of weight gain.

To figure the approximate number of calories to maintain weight loss for a woman who is 115 pounds, we multiply 115 by 12, which gives us 1,380 calories per day, or 9,660 a week. To figure the approximate number of calories for a man to maintain, let's multiply 160 by 15, which gives him 2,400 calories per day or 16,800 per week.

Weight

You also need to know how much you weigh over a week's time. It is impossible to maintain an absolute weight on a day-to-day basis. It is possible, however, and most practical, to stay within that Goal Range most of the time.

The scale is the instrument you will use to measure your status. It is an equal partner to your eating plan in the maintenance process. You have to pledge that you will trust the information your instrument gives you. Keep informed regularly. Preferably daily. Not less than weekly.

The Great Weight Maintenance Experiments

You've reached your goal weight. And now comes a time of testing. What can you eat? Anything? How much? The following are three experiments to give you a start on your own maintenance scriptwriting. These have been helpful to many. But maintenance is an individual matter, so you may wish to alter any given plan so that it makes sense in your life.

One experiment of maintenance is to stay on the diet that worked for you before and add foods each day within a calorie limit or by units. A variation of that theme for Wild Weekend Dieters would be to increase Wild Weekend Units on Saturday and Sunday and stay on the Weekday Slimdown Plan during the week. Or the Core Diet. The WSP is a menu expression of the Core Diet.

A second experiment calls for you to set a calorie limit for each day and to just stop eating when you reach that limit. This works for many people. A variation of this theme is to keep track of calories and keep them low during the week and have a "free" weekend.

Or you may want to try a combination of the experiments above and keep your calories low, low, low, Monday through Friday. Give yourself the weekends "free," with no thought to calories or to Wild Weekend Units.

As frustrating and anxiety-provoking as this experimenting may be, it is a necessary information-gathering step so that you can establish the food and situational limits for your thin future. You can do it! You have already established through your initial weight loss that you have strength and resolve.

The length of this testing phase is not fixed by the calendar. Diet arithmetic is frustrating; it doesn't add up or subtract down on anything that might resemble a precise schedule. You may learn what you need to know in six months, or it may take you two years. You know it's over when you experience the relief from anxiety around food and eating that comes from knowing exactly what you have to do to be thin forever and that you have made peace with those limits. You have also come to the realization that food is not a treat that you give yourself; it is the fuel your body needs to keep going.

To Find Out Along the Weigh

Which foods and drinks are really important to you?

Are there some foods that come with such a high-calorie price tag that they're not worth the purchase?

Do you know which foods trigger miseating for you?

Give Yourself a Break

As you progress with your experiments and expand your food limits, you may come to a hard place. Without warning, bad eating habits, poor control, and thoughtless behavior make an appearance, and unexpected weight gains show on the scale.

It is an important part of the long-term success process for you to give yourself permission to be imperfect. You didn't become a Diet Angel when you lost your weight; no one is. Angels don't have to diet. We do. And occasionally we all slip. We take the easy way—like eating the butter on the fish we ordered dry or eating more than we intended to or eating something we didn't really want or didn't plan for.

When you miseat without thought, reflect back on this incident. Replay and analyze it. What caused it? There's always a reason. You can depend on this. Decide what you will do the next time you are in a similar situation. Write yourself a new ending to the scene. This time stay in control; this time you win. Then congratulate yourself for being able to do the replay because it is *this* kind of attention, *this* kind of discipline that saw you through the weight-loss process and that is now insurance for your thin future.

Tips for You the Maintainer

- Keep foods that are hard for you to handle out of your house. You don't need to be a pillar of willpower; you need to be thin.
- Work those foods and drinks that are really important to you into your personal maintenance plan.
- Exercise does burn up calories. Consider adding movement to your life.
- Learn the calorie content of the foods you especially like or eat often.
- Keep a Food Diary.
- Keep a weight chart.
- Emphasize the sociability aspect of eating out and of parties rather than the food.
- Give away your fat clothes. Or burn them. Getting rid of them is a must.
- Dress for the new you. Toss out old, dull clothes.
- Change your hairstyle and, if you're a woman, your makeup.
- Invest the energy that you had for dieting in a new interest.
- Keep a journal and record the feelings you're experiencing around food and eating.

As you buckle on your white belt to begin again as a maintainer, remember that you are not really back to the beginning. For each time you start again, you bring to the new experience information about yourself and about the subject; in this case, healthy eating and weight loss, and you bring your success experience.

As you set out on your thin life remind yourself frequently that you have accomplished something important and valuable for yourself. Something difficult. Give yourself full credit. You are a black belt, an achiever on the highest level of skill.